E.E. CLEVELAND

Let the Church Roll On

AN AUTOBIOGRAPHY

Pacific Press Publishing Association
Nampa, Idaho
Oshawa, Ontario, Canada

Edited by Sophie Anderson and Kenneth R. Wade
Designed by Michelle C. Petz
Photos courtesy of Oakwood College

Copyright ©1997 by
Pacific Press Publishing Association
Printed in the United States
All Rights Reserved

ISBN 0-8163-1383-0

Contents

Chapter 1	Kidnapped	9
Chapter 2	The Ninth Inning	15
Chapter 3	Jacob's Ladder	19
Chapter 4	In Black and White	27
Chapter 5	Tough Love	31
Chapter 6	Lighting Torches	37
Chapter 7	The King and I	43
Chapter 8	Panther Permit	49
Chapter 9	Instrument of Change	55
Chapter 10	Modern Miracle	67
Chapter 11	Washington	73
Chapter 12	Oh Yeah!	81
Chapter 13	Where Shall I Go?	85
Chapter 14	The King's Palace	91
Chapter 15	Detroit, 1966	99
Chapter 16	Overseas	105
Chapter 17	Oakwood College	111
Chapter 18	The Gifts	115
Chapter 19	Roots	119
Chapter 20	Poem—Tell It	123

Philosophy

"I have seen God, for so long,
do so much, with so little,
I now believe He can do anything
with nothing—meaning **me**."

Dedication

To Edward Earl Cleveland II
and Omar Clifford Cleveland,
my grandsons,
who have brought me so much joy—
I dedicate this book.

Introduction

This book is the product of fifty-three years of preaching the gospel on six continents of the earth. It is the gospel of Christ in capsule form, written for busy people. The writer recognizes that some will read this book who are burdened beyond their capacity to survive. They need no lengthy presentation of the theology of salvation. They need a lifeline now. This small loaf of bread of life is for them. The author's prayer is that, like the five biscuits and two fishes of Scripture, these simple words will be blessed to achieve results that are above and beyond the natural.

E. E. Cleveland

1

Kidnapped

Wartrace was a sleepy little farming town in Tennessee. William Cleveland, Sr., found job opportunities in nearby Chattanooga more attractive. He and his wife traveled daily to the city, dropped their young son, Bill, off at school, and went to their respective jobs. The wife worked at a grocery store next to the school. After school hours, young Bill, aged nine, played near the store until his mother closed up. Then the father would pick them up and take them home.

One afternoon Bill failed to check in at the store after school. The kidnapper, Henry Duncan, saw Bill playing alone in the playground, wrapped the boy in an overcoat, and ran to his own house. The Duncans, a well-to-do couple, desperately wanted a child. Bill's parents passed, more than once, the house where he was confined looking for their son, but the search was fruitless. Raising Bill as their own child, the Duncans renamed him Henry Duncan, Jr. His parents never saw their son again, and his mother died of a broken heart. Bill's new parents were kind to him and willed him their house at their death. He vaguely remembered some men standing around him arguing for him to sign a paper. When he did, he discovered too late that they had tricked him out of his house.

While my mother called my father "Henry" until he died, he never forgot his original name—William Clifford Cleveland. With this name he grew to manhood, married, and went to war.

The booming guns of World War I fell silent. William Clifford Cleveland of Chattanooga, Tennessee, served in the bloody contest. He was pushing with General Pershing's forces deep into Europe when the good news came: The armistice was signed on November 11, 1918, and the victorious allied armies were going home.

Bill Cleveland had survived the global struggle unscathed and was eager to resume a life of normalcy with his wife, Eunice, and two-year-old son, William James. Like thousands of other Americans, he bore the heavy heartbreak of parting and laughed with the joy of reunion. Earl, another son, was born. When seven years passed, bringing the third son, Harold Lovell, the Cleveland family was complete.

Bill had met Eunice at a high-school football game. Streaking toward the end zone for a touchdown, he noticed this pretty girl cheering for him on the sidelines. He had to meet her after the game. Introducing himself, he offered to carry her schoolbooks home. When he reached her house, he felt that a modest kiss on the cheek was in order. She slapped him so hard that he fell to the ground. Sitting there, put in his place, he decided she was the girl for him. He vowed to marry her. He did. They were married in 1916.

When Bill entered the army, circumstances tested his faith in God early. As a Seventh-day Adventist Christian, not only was he a conscientious objector, but he refused to work on the Sabbath as well. He made it clear to his superior officers that he would not carry a gun but that he would go into any battle to save lives as a medical corpsman. His fellow soldiers, annoyed by his convictions, decided to give him a sand bath to change his mind. This painful prank consisted of rubbing sand over the body surface until the victim is raw with pain. The misery would last for weeks.

Entering the barracks to grab him, they swarmed toward him, only to find Cleveland on his knees in prayer. The room fell silent. Slowly they retreated in respect. No one had to convince him that God answers prayers.

His sergeant decided that Cleveland was going to work on the Sabbath. This young private couldn't get away with special treatment. Early on Sabbath morning, the sergeant took Cleveland to a remote spot. Six soldiers aimed rifles at his head.

"You have one minute to pick up the shovel and work, soldier," the sergeant ordered. Cleveland waited for the shot.

"Take the shovel!" barked the officer.

"I can't, sir," he replied.

"Cleveland," shouted the sergeant, "I'm going to hand you this shovel. If you don't take it and it falls to the ground, you die. Now take it!"

12 · Let the Church Roll On

Cleveland stood there, deep in prayer, expecting each moment to be his last. When he didn't take the shovel, the sergeant propped it against his body. It crashed to the ground. The noise boomed like the sound of six rifles. His heart beat wildly. There was silence. He pinched himself. Was he still alive?

"To your barracks, soldier. Prepare for court-martial."

His body aching with relief, he trotted to his room. Falling on his knees, he praised the God of Heaven for his deliverance.

The day of the court-martial, the officers assembled and made charges against him. Bill Cleveland stood erect before the officers of the court, his Bible strong and comforting in hand. "Soldier," said the general, "give us a reason for the hope that is within you."

For forty full minutes, Bill Cleveland taught the Sabbath to the generals, who sat in rapt attention. At the end of his presentation, the commanding officer dismissed the other officers, brought a chair to the table, and sat facing my father.

"Soldier," he said. " I know you people. I have a Seventh-day Adventist maid. Take your Sabbaths off, but don't teach that to any other soldiers in my outfit. Dismissed!"

From this faithful foundation—a quiet Christian mother and a father who stood like a giant oak at the head of his family—the three Cleveland boys were raised. The church was the center of our culture. We all went to prayer meeting, and Sabbath morning found us in Sabbath School. We were trained to be leaders as deliberately as a tree is planted and groomed. That William, Jr., would become president of the Southwest Region Conference should have surprised no one. That Harold would become president of the Allegheny West Conference was a foregone conclusion. Both men served with distinction as pastors before their election to executive office. *Would I too experience executive privilege? Would I also serve as pastor, staying quiet in a small church?* I wondered. God's plan for my life would be different. I would not experience executive privilege, but I would be called to world responsibility. The earth would be my pulpit. Writing these words at seventy-five, fifty-four years of gospel ministry leave a legacy behind me. It has not ended yet.

2

The Ninth Inning

I was born on March 11, 1921, in Huntsville, Alabama. The future seemed to offer little to Bill Cleveland's sons, but Daddy and Mother didn't seem to know it. Daddy worked three jobs, sixteen hours a day, for as long as I can remember. He always drove some kind of a truck. He forbade us to ride the buses and streetcars because they were segregated. This meant walking to school and back, a fifteen-mile journey, five days a week. Dad couldn't drive us, for he needed the truck for work. On Sabbaths, since the truck could not carry everyone, we walked to and from church, six miles round trip. I later learned that my rugged health and that of my brothers was partly due to this walking regimen.

My parents trained us early to work, a character-building exercise. We helped our father with his janitorial duties at the Girls' Preparatory School. We also sold coal, kindling, and even snow cones. Because of our strong work ethic, we were never homeless, hungry, or ill-clothed. During the Great Depression of the 30s, we lived well, for everybody did his part. We were taught never to be ashamed of honest labor, however menial. During the Depression, my father would contract with the large grocery chains to take the perishable vegetables and distribute them to our neighbors free of charge. There was no shortage of goodwill in the neighborhood for the Clevelands. Because of my parents' willingness to feed strangers and stranded travelers, our home became famous as the hospitality house. Students traveling to and from Oakwood College took their "layovers" in Chattanooga. Mysteriously, they always had our phone number. My father, the neighborhood daddy, would often load the truck with youngsters on Sunday and take us to the nearest open field for baseball and a fun-filled day of sports.

Early in life my parents noticed that I had a weakness that could threaten my future security. While I was an enthusiastic "starter," I seldom completed any task. Something had to be done. To cure this problem, my parents conspired with Miss Tommie Duffy, the head of the Girls' Preparatory School, an Irish lady, to employ me for the summer at her house on Lookout Mountain. Most tourists went to Lookout Mountain for pleasure and relaxation, but my weekly trips up the "steepest incline railway in the world" were a painful experience. Miss Duffy was tough. There was no promise of wages, just three months of backbreaking toil. When the work was done, my taskmaster invented new things to do. She tried to teach me to wait tables, but that plan flopped when I accidentally touched the back of the neck of

The Ninth Inning · 17

an important Chattanooga official with a hot aluminum chicken platter.

"Earl will make a poor servant," Miss Duffy told my father.

When we ran out of legitimate work, my employer sent me into a large field with a short-handled sickle. "Level the grass," she ordered.

"This is ridiculous," I moaned, swinging the sickle. Suddenly I heard a noise of something dropping from a tree. I looked up from my kneeling position into the face of an angry snake, bent on punishing me for being there without his permission. Some have asked me what kind of snake it was. I didn't stay for an interview. Dropping the sickle, I tore madly from the area—never to return.

"Go back and get the sickle," Miss Duffy said.

"No way." My resolution was firm. Miss Duffy had discovered my "bottom line." Snakes and I have nothing in common. The mere sight of one is enough to pump my adrenaline and move my feet.

Then I was sent to clean a room. Working carefully, I did everything I knew to complete the job. At last I knew the room was clean. Miss Duffy came in to inspect. She could find nothing wrong. "Bring me a chair," she said. Standing on it, she rubbed her finger across the top of the high windowsill. Her white finger came up black with dirt. Her verbal scolding withered my pride.

One summer with Miss Duffy, and I was cured. I became a finisher of the first magnitude. I breezed through my weekends at home with its miniscule duties. I never forgot

18 · Let the Church Roll On

Miss Duffy and what she taught me. I think of her often with deep appreciation. She made me stronger in "the ninth inning" than in the first. I learned from her that the fourth quarter is the most important of all. Miss Duffy not only taught me an enduring lesson, but she further encouraged me in the path of success by paying my entrance fee at Oakwood College.

3

Jacob's Ladder

Howard High School in Chattanooga, Tennessee, was the school for Blacks in those early years. W. J. Davenport was an inspiring giant in the educational system. His teachers taught us the authorized curriculum, but then they would teach Black history and culture. They made us *learn*. Mr. Brown and Mr. Bradley stretched our minds to the breaking point. At graduation, W. T. Lyons and I shared the valedictorian honors, and I was designated commencement speaker.

As president of the senior class, I was supposed to lead the grand march at the junior-senior prom. I informed my class sponsor that I could not attend, because I did not believe in dancing. I was excused on grounds of conscience. Mrs. Pryor taught me mathematics. I will never forget her stern countenance and cryptic manner. When I was lacking in enthusiasm for learning, she would invoke the memory of my parents, who stood ready and willing to apply corporal

20 · Let the Church Roll On

punishment stimuli when necessary.

From the age of six I was aware of my call to preach the gospel. My childhood ministry crossed denominational lines. I was a "boy preacher" in Chattanooga. I have never wanted to be anything but a preacher. Preachers have been my heroes. Their power in the Black community is phenomenal; their variety of function is mind-boggling. Politicians covet their power. But what impresses me most is their persuasive power, their ability to be used of the Almighty to change lives for the better. To facilitate the reordering of priorities in the lives of the unfulfilled is ministry of the highest order. To bring hope to the disconsolate, peace to the troubled, and light to dispel the darkness from sin-tortured lives, became, and remains, my supreme passion.

I grew up in the Fortwood section of Chattanooga. We lived on a hill overlooking Enlanger Hospital to the north and Engle Stadium to the east. "The Whites Only" line was a half block south of us uphill. White boys played ball with us in an open field "on the line." For years, we children knew no difference except "the line." When I was about fourteen, it happened. Nobody in the Black community knew exactly who passed the word to the White kids, but it was passed. We were suddenly "niggers." And, of course, we fought. For some strange reason, we were under persona nongrata, and the Whites abandoned the field to us.

There were two city parks, Lincoln Park for Blacks and Central Park for Whites. And, of course, there was always Lookout Mountain. Black folk worked there, White folk lived there. Come sundown, Blacks rode the incline down. The park for Whites had more and better equipment and always got the best, but I was too busy enjoying what we had in the park for Blacks to care. I was in high school when I learned that we were being taxed equally, but our money was passing through White hands to White projects.

As I was growing up, the threat of violence was ever-present in the neighborhood. Three of my best friends were gunned down. Others went to prison. Saturday night was the night to survive. Liquor flowed freely, and the blaring sound of searing jazz filled the air. The smells of frying fish and barbecue steamed heavy in the atmosphere. There were Black policemen in our neighborhood. When I was a child, the paddywagon was a fact of life. My memory is still vivid of "Bull" Dawson, the feared Black cop, taming the unruly. My father rented a stand in Lincoln Park, where we sold "cool-outs." It seemed we spent as much time dodging bullets as serving the customers.

For most of us kids, though, life was good. The neighborhood raised the children. We played, worked, fought, and dreamed. There were the silver-tongued orators who told us that we could make it. There were the teachers who prodded us to "stretch ourselves to our limits to achieve." There were the preachers who trained us for leadership, lifted our moral sights, and declared us capable of the unimaginable.

Of course, there were our parents who bore us up on wings of prayer and kept us focused on the stars while we strove to conquer the "here and now." That would not be easy!

Oakwood College was my Mecca, a place for spiritual

development and ministerial training. Though self-expression was never a problem with me, it was Elder Calvin Moseley who taught me to organize my thoughts and present them so they would be understood and remembered. History repeated itself, and I was elected president of my graduating class at Oakwood College.

"How are you doing in school?" my father asked me on one of my visits home. I cited my academic progress.

"I mean socially," he said, interrupting.

"I haven't seen any young lady on campus that met my standards," I answered.

"Have you paused to consider how little you have to offer?"

Sobered by this question, I returned and found a most satisfactory solution—Celia Marie Abney. I had come to the campus seeking an angel and found only human beings. After the encounter with my dad, I returned, searching for a human being and found an angel. Upon graduating from Oakwood College, I was not assigned to an internship by a conference. It seems that my instructors were not as impressed with me as I was with them, and so no one hired me. I watched, uncomprehending, while my classmates went to their assignments. I stood expectant but was passed by. Elder W. R. Robinson invited me to help him in a tent revival in Columbus, Ohio. I eagerly accepted. At the end of the highly successful revival, the questions remained. *Where would I go? What would I do?*

The Ohio conference committee met and hired three young preachers, all White. Again I was passed by because "there was no colored money." My friends, the Robinsons, suggested that I go to a small town to prove my worth. I went to Toledo, Ohio, and presented myself to the small congregation. They were glad to see me, and during the six months that I spent there, the members gave me strong encouragement. I stayed with a saint named David Washington. He was a religious-book salesman and well versed in the Scriptures. Every morning at 5:00 a.m. he would waken me for worship. We would sing:

> The men that love and fear Thy name
> Shall see their hopes fulfilled;
> The mighty God will compass them
> With favor as a shield.
> —*Seventh-day Adventist Hymnal, 39.*

These words fed my dreams of one day having a pastorate and saving souls. The winter was severe for my hope, and I fought to keep it alive. I grew desperate.

"Lord," I prayed one night, "I will neither eat nor sleep until I receive an appointment to the ministry." I promptly fell off to sleep. I was awakened by the doorbell. It was a telegram from my father. It read, "Carolina Conference offers internships. Will you accept?" I fired off a one-word telegram reply— "Accepted." I would learn later of the miracle that had occurred.

While I was in Toledo, Ohio, working, praying, and fasting for some form of ministerial recognition, the Carolina Conference committee was meeting in Chattanooga, Tennessee, to select a young Black candidate for one of its pulpits. The leading candidate was talented, a great preacher, and would have a distinguished career as a lay activities secretary-treasurer of a conference and chief administrator of Riverside Hospital. But at the time, there was one opening for the job, and he was the one man recommended. It was expected to be a routine appointment. Hundreds of miles away, with no contact with anyone but God, I did not even know that the committee was meeting. As the discussion moved toward the decision stage, Elder N. B. Smith blurted out my name. He later told me that my name flashed into his mind at that crucial moment.

"Earl Cleveland," he uttered with a force that surprised him, "I can't vote until you interview him." At that point, Matthew Green interrupted, "Neither will I vote until you talk to Earl." The president of the conference, eager to get on with the business, asked where I was.

"I don't know," Elder Smith replied, "but I will ask his daddy." I learned later that the White conference president wanted the other candidate but agreed to the delay in deference to brethren Smith and Green. Three months passed before I was summoned to Charlotte for the crucial interview. Meanwhile, my older brother, Bill, hired me to teach school in Paducah, Kentucky, for those three long months.

The letter from Charlotte with the bus ticket finally arrived, and I was on my way. Upon my arrival in Charlotte, I was whisked to the conference office for interrogation. Assigned a place in the center of the circle of chairs, I sat, the conference staff of all White males around me. They took turns questioning me.

"You will preach tomorrow at the colored church. Then you will return to Kentucky to await our decision," the president solemnly announced at the end. The decision had already been made in heaven, but Charlotte had not yet gotten the word. But it would not be long in coming. Before noon the next day, Charlotte would know.

The Sabbath day of my redemption dawned clear, except for a few fleecy clouds against an azure blue sky—a day bright with promise. The conference brethren came early with their families. They sat directly in front of the pulpit. That was a mistake. It put them directly in my line of fire.

Finally, the Black brothers and sisters assembled, in varying stages of skepticism. I was "lean and green," and my ill-fitting clerical attire did little to heighten anticipation. After a very brief introduction by the president, special music, and a solo, I would get my chance. But not yet. The sister who sang evidently believed that her musical offering would be the sole soul food of the day, so she sang until her ability to produce and our capacity to receive were depleted. Then only was I allowed to preach.

"Can a Man Be Perfect?" I preached. Twenty minutes into the sermon, Black folk were shouting, and the White folk were crying and trying not to shout. Jehovah knocked down the door and led me into the organized ministry on the wings of a sermon. I would not look back. I was on my way. Or was I?

"You'll hear from me within three weeks," the president said when he took me to the bus station and sent me back to Kentucky. I did. I was ordered to begin my internship June 2, 1942. I was numb with joy—a joy that I would never lose!

4

In Black and White

Chattanooga, Tennessee, is just thirty miles from Southern Missionary College (now called Southern College). My father, a vegetarian, used to drive there to buy vegetarian foods. One day while there, I asked my daddy if this was the college that I would attend. I did not know then what I know now. The school was segregated and did not even have a Black janitor. I resolved then and there that I would give my church no rest until this evil was resolved, and I have kept that promise. I am at rest. I would live to deal with Southern College and help them over this hurdle. I was a part of the human relations group in Washington who outlawed all forms of racism and discrimination in all Adventist institutions wherever. Southern College, however, got my personal attention. It happened like this.

When Dr. Lorenzo Grant was a staff member at Southern College, his mother died. I had baptized Mrs. Grant years ago in St. Louis. Church policy had, at this point in time, opened the school to members of all races, and Dr. Grant was a Black faculty member. "Will you deliver her eulogy?" he asked.

"Yes," I agreed. "Where will you hold the service?"

"In Chattanooga."

"Why not use the Southern College Campus Church?" I asked. He promised to check it out. He called me later and said that the board had agreed. "Where will you bury her?" I asked.

"In Chattanooga," he answered.

"Why don't you integrate the graveyard out there in Collegedale?" I asked.

"I'll check it out," he answered. He called back later. "We'll bury her out here." So it happened history was made in the staid Collegedale community. A Black preacher delivered the eulogy. Black morticians officiated. Mrs. Grant integrated a White Collegedale graveyard, and the angels smiled.

In the year 1950, the church elected me to the Union Conference level. This meant that I would sit on the Union Conference committee. I attended my first Union committee meeting at Southern Missionary College. At mealtime, Elder V. G. Anderson announced a recess until two o'clock. Immediately the line formed to enter the cafeteria. I got in the line with everybody else. The six Black brothers, however, remained sitting in their places in the boardroom. How was I to know that no Blacks had ever eaten in that college cafeteria before? It was only then that I noticed I was the only Black person in the line. At this point, I caught sight of the face of the Union president. For what seemed an eternity, we looked one another in the face. He blinked, returned to the boardroom, and ordered all the other Blacks into the line. History was made that day, and Collegedale has never been the same.

Shortly after my election to the General Conference, I was invited to the Florida Conference for a two-day workers' meeting. I would lecture for thirteen hours on this assignment. The meeting was held in the chapel of the Florida Hospital in Orlando, still segregated. As noon hour approached, I announced that I would have to cut the lecture short as I needed to bring my wife and son to the cafeteria for lunch. A look of consternation filled the faces of my listeners, and the Union president slipped out of the room. He returned shortly, and I finished my lecture. With a troubled look on his face, he asked to speak with me privately. "Cleveland," he said, "I have a problem. The manager of the hospital says that if you enter the cafeteria, he will close it down."

"Tell him to prepare to shut it down, for I fully intend to enter."

"But can't we work something out?" he asked.

"Like what?"

"Well, we don't want to disturb these good meetings. If you and your family will eat elsewhere, and you finish your assignment, I will have the manager's job before sundown tomorrow, and the new manager will get things straight." We shook hands on the bargain. He kept his word. The new manager desegregated the whole hospital. Today, Florida Hospital is a model of colorblind ministry. About once a

30 · Let the Church Roll On

year I stop by to eat in their very colorful cafeteria, and smile. As I see men and women of all races functioning in their respective disciplines, I wonder if they will ever appreciate those privileges, so long denied, that are now theirs.

Oakwood College, in Huntsville, Alabama, was the college of my choice. My brother Bill had graduated from the school, and it filled my dreams of campus heaven. Operated by the General Conference of Seventh-day Adventists for the training of Black students, it was dedicated to the training of the heart, head, and hand. Established in 1896, Oakwood College has become a full-fledged liberal arts college, an accredited member of the United Negro College Fund Family.

In 1939 I arrived on campus, becoming a member of the freshman class. My experience was highlighted by the teaching, example, and charisma of C. E. Moseley. In his youth, there was no better. His sermonic style and substance was electric.

There at Oakwood, I found and married "the light of my life," Celia Marie Abney. As of this writing, she has been my wife for fifty-one years. She has sustained a world ministry by God's grace, besides having a ministry of her own. Aside from the duties of wife and mother, she visited the unsaved, played the piano, passed out literature, and cooked for the evangelistic company. She is, and has been, a counselor to thousands, a school teacher, and music instructor. After graduating from Oakwood College, we were married May 29, 1943.

5

Tough Love

After camp meeting, I began what became a lifelong hunt for lost souls. I went to Ashboro, North Carolina, and persuaded the principal of the high school to let me begin some religion-educational lectures there. He let me in for four weeks. I preached and was blessed with sixteen precious souls for baptism. Since I had disappeared from the conference radar screen for one month, they didn't know where I was until I surfaced with a request for baptismal assistance. They reprimanded me for making unauthorized forays into another man's district. In defense, I cited our Lord's command: "Go ye into all the world and preach the gospel to every creature." They reminded me that "all the world" meant where the church sent me and that I would have to leave some of the world to someone else. They reminded me that unless they knew where I was, they could not send me my monthly check. Later in my experience, when I had preached for eight months and received no check, I wondered if the treasurer had wandered "into all the world" but had forgotten my section.

I was then ordered to High Point, North Carolina, told to proceed to a certain vacant lot, and when the truck came with the tent, "stay with it." I took them literally. When the four big bags of canvas hit the ground, I slept on top of them all night. Like Nebuchadnezzar, my brow was wet with the dew of heaven when the boss appeared. Elder H. D Singleton was stunned that I had stayed up all night but promptly put me to work for the rest of the day.

My three months under his tutelage were an unmixed blessing. Having mastered the mechanics of evangelism, he faithfully taught me what he knew. Being naturally inquisitive, our periods of discussions were long and frequent. His personal integrity shone through all he did. Later, he became an official of the world conference of SDAs. Many years later, I would join him there.

My first pastorate was in the city of Fayetteville, North Carolina. Lumberton and Laurinburg were added to complete my district. Since evangelism was and is my first love, I couldn't stay in a church. I pitched my tent. A young white evangelist named Billy Graham was just beginning his illustrious career in the same state. The world would hear from both of us, for God would use each in His own way.

I must confess that the traditional pastorate held little appeal for me. Evangelism was in my blood. The tent was my favorite auditorium. A storm blew down my first tent three days before my grand opening. As the people arrived for the meeting, my tent was still on the ground. It was still raining. My associate and I stood in the rain explaining to those who came that we would open next week. I was not encouraged by some of the comments.

"I'm glad I wasn't in there when the thing blew down," said one.

"That old man must not be right with God, or the tent wouldn't have fallen," said another. My associate, Silas McClamb, must have wondered at that point if God had led him to be there. At my request, he had quit a good-paying job to come to Fayetteville to work with me. He would later distinguish himself as publishing secretary of the South Atlantic Conference and later of the Northeastern Conference. But now we were in Fayetteville, staring at the bleak beginnings of my evangelistic career that would span fifty-four years.

Quitting never occurred to us. We worked the next few days with feverish activity. The tent was finally repaired and pitched, the platform built, the piano rented, the chairs put in place, the new advertisement distributed, and we were ready to go. On opening night, fifteen people came. After much prayer, we gave those fifteen people the full treatment. The powers of God anointed human effort, and the crowd grew.

My wife organized a youth choir of about thirty voices. I started a radio broadcast over station WFNC, which lasted for over two years. This choir supplied the music. At the end of the campaign, eighty-four people were baptized, including the choir. The program lasted three months. I preached six nights per week for twelve weeks and twice on the Sabbaths of the last six weeks. Those were the days.

After taking down the tent, we continued on Sunday nights in the church. Feeding the church attendance with the radio broadcast, we baptized all winter so that the churches were packed three nights per week and on the Sabbath.

One Sunday night during the tent meetings, two people who had sat in different sections of the audience approached me hesitantly. "Who was that preacher who came in and sat down when you stood up to preach?" they asked.

"There is only one chair up there and I sat in that."

"Yes, but when you stood up to preach, he came in, knelt briefly to pray, sat in your seat, and vigorously supported your preaching," they said. It suddenly dawned on me that a person, invisible to me but visible to them, had occupied the podium with me and endorsed my ministry. I have no doubt, as I write these lines, that an angel of God was sent to endorse the beginning of an evangelistic career that would span six continents and lead thousands of all races to the foot of the cross.

Church officials were determined that I would learn pastoral skills. Each new city entered added to my string of churches to pastor. At one time, I pastored Durham, Raleigh, Fayetteville, Lumberton, and Laurinburg. My intensive summer campaigns did not exempt me from raising the annual conference assessments: House visitation, funerals, marriages, and other pastoral responsibilities. In fact, I carried three carloads of singers to a certain city during the annual Ingathering-solicitation program. The police arrested all of them for soliciting without a permit. The chief finally found me in one of the neighborhoods and hauled me in too.

As we entered the lockup, we could hear singing coming from the courtroom. "Rev, follow me. Let's see what's going on," the chief said. As we entered the courtroom, my wife was leading my members in a concert for all the jailers, clerks, and secretaries. My folk had arrested the jailers with their music and testimonies.

"You win, Rev," the chief said. "Now get your people out of town as fast as you can, so we can get back to normal. And don't come back!" We had sung our way out of jail.

However, not all the work of the Lord was that risky. Our radio ministry, begun in Fayetteville in 1943, had expanded to Raleigh, Durham, Greensboro, and Winston-Salem, with large numbers of young people singing their way into the church in my wife's youth choirs. We conducted large "feed the hungry" programs in over fifty cities. Grocery stores would give a variety of foods for this purpose, and people attending the services would bring canned foods. Medical people donated their services to the needy. Dr. Carl Dent was especially helpful for many years in this "pro bono" effort.

Thousands of young people responded to our soul-winning programs. Fifty-four years later, many of them are still alive, and I am teaching their children in college. Many are holding responsible positions in the church and the world. This is a source of great joy to us.

Church administrators soon decided that evangelism was, and is, my passion and relieved me of all pastoral responsi-

36 · Let the Church Roll On

bilities. I was promoted to the conference staff position of conference evangelist. Any false pride in the promotion, however, was dashed in a taxicab when the driver, a friendly fellow, asked me, "What kind of work do you do?"

"I'm a preacher," I replied.

"Where is your church?"

"I don't have a church," I smiled.

"Oh, you're an evangelist preacher?"

"Yes, that's it." There was a moment of silence. Then the driver spoke.

"Cheer up, Rev, your luck will change."

Praise the Lord. My luck never did.

6

Lighting Torches

In 1950 I was elected to the Union-Conference level of my church. This gave me access to the states of Georgia, Florida, North and South Carolina, Tennessee, Kentucky, Alabama, and Mississippi. For four years I worked as an evangelist, summer and winter. My wife shared my appetite for this work and followed me from city to city without complaint.

We had bought a trailer in 1948 and lived in it contentedly for two and a half years.

"We are just like the turtle," Celia said one day while we were moving to the next city. "Our house is on our backs." I understood what she meant. We soon sold the trailer and rented a home. Her delight made it all worthwhile. She deserved it. After our marriage, we had "roomed" with homeowners, enduring all of its inconveniences. When we roomed with non-Adventists, the hazards multiplied.

It always seemed that our "landlords" would attend my meetings on nights when unpopular Bible messages were scheduled. The next day, we would hear the dreaded words: "You will have to move. We need the room." This happened four times in one year. We learned early to "endure—like good soldiers." This was a small price to pay for soul-seeking.

Church administration decided early to add ministerial training to my portfolio. My soul-winning campaigns were designated "field schools." Under this academic umbrella, Andrews University and Oakwood College would send ministerial students to me for training. As of this writing, over sixteen hundred ministers worldwide have had the "Cleveland Treatment." To me, these young men were a trust from God, and each was a brother. They had access to my food and home at all hours. It has been our joy to watch them grow and go. They have gone on to become evangelists, pastors, administrators, and educators. And they have not forgotten. Willie Lewis and Ralph Peay were baptized in the early years of my ministry. They became conference presidents. Elders Sandy Robinson, Robert LaGrone, and T. J. Jackson were baptized in Mobile, Alabama, and made records in the literature ministry. Ira Harrel, J. P. Willis, and Joseph Hinson made their marks in departmental work at the conference level. Fred Nealey and Leslie Pollard have had distinguished pastorates. William Dawson has served well in the pastoral, and Welton Jones continues to set records in publishing. It was my privilege to baptize all of the above and to witness the Holy Spirit in their ministry. I also baptized Earl

Howard, whose two sons now distinguish themselves in the ministry.

In my congregation in Greensboro, North Carolina, was a young future dentist named C. D. Brooks. His mother was a devout Seventh-day Adventist and his father a staunch Methodist Christian. Father Brooks faithfully attended my public meetings. One evening as young C. D. sat in the tent, the Holy Spirit visited him with power. The benediction was said, the tent emptied, but the young teenager just sat there. He was under arrest by a power higher than himself. After that night, the only dentistry involving him would be that performed on him. He would be a preacher. This meant a switch in his plans for an education from A & T College, Greensboro, to Oakwood College in Huntsville, Alabama. When his father heard of the change, he was angry and declared that he would not pay a penny on his education bill. Three weeks later, I baptized his father. C. D. Brooks was on his way to fame as the speaker on the *Breath of Life* telecast.

It is seldom that one has the privilege of field training his own brother. How could I know that H. L. Cleveland, seven years my junior, would distinguish himself as an evangelist, pastor, church builder, and conference president? The Berean Seventh-day Adventist Church in Atlanta and the contemporary structure in Savannah, Georgia, are monuments to his building skills.

During his pastorates, packed houses were a testament to his preaching power. In Ocala, Florida, he baptized over one hundred people in ten weeks. Slipping into town one night when he was preaching, I found him operating in a couple of army dormitory tents sewn together. The place was packed, with scores standing outside. In Atlanta, Georgia, he baptized nearly one thousand people, built the Berean church, then headed north. After successfully pastoring the Glenville church in Cleveland, Ohio, and adding over five hundred members to its church rolls, he was elected president of the Allegheny West Conference, a position he held for eleven years.

I could experience no greater joy than seeing the power of God exhibited in the ministry of the young men who worked with me. George Rainey, Leonard Newton, E. C. Ward, Warren Banfield, Richard Barron, and Lucius Daniels were among them. M. T. Battle was originally hired at my insistence and went on to serve faithfully and efficiently in the secretariat of the world body. Benjamin Reaves became president of Oakwood College. James Edgecombe became president of the Southeastern Conference. Elbert Shepperd became vice president of the Pacific Union Conference, and William Scales became secretary of evangelism for all of North America. Wintley Phipps became a world-renowned minister of music. Delbert Baker became editor of *Message* magazine. John Street became president of the City Council of Philadelphia, Pennsylvania.

In the early days of my ministry, I heard of another young minister on the rise as an evangelist, Billy Graham. What a great one he became, leading untold millions to Christ. His clean living, straightforward message propelled him into the John Wesley, Charles Spurgeon, and Dwight Moody category. Though our paths never crossed, we were aware of each other. A letter from one of our leaders in Brazil quotes him as complimenting my preaching of the gospel. It is no secret that I regard Billy as the foremost gospel preacher of this age.

Other musical greats have enriched my ministry through the years. T. Marshall Kelly traveled with me throughout the United States and Australia. His rich bass voice so charmed the Australians that they renamed him "Okelly" and had him returned to Australia with his wife for his own unique ministry. Then there was Charles Lee Brooks, the tenor. Over a period of twenty years, he always added his unique talent to my preaching ministry. Miss Joyce Bryant, world-class entertainer, never refused my invitations to help with her music and Christian visitation. Her velvet voice moved many to the foot of the cross. Little Richard left the entertainment world and for years gave a powerful witness to God's saving grace. During those days, he was never too busy to grace our meetings. Clifton Davis came repeatedly to add his talent to the glory and the cause of God. Samuel Thomas was one of my early trainees who had a distinguished career as union departmental secretary. Donnie Ross received his call to preach under my ministry. Elder Harvey Kibble insisted that I train all four of his sons: Harvey, Alvin, Harold, and Herman. All four have had outstanding successes in the ministry. George Earle began his ministry with me in 1948. Emmanuel Chester served in five campaigns.

Outstanding women have made their mark as Bible instructors in city after city. Lillie Evans, Ola May Harris, Mildred Johnson, Bertha Bailey, Ellen Anderson, Vivian Perry, and Beatrice Hampton brought hundreds to the foot of the cross in my campaigns.

7

The King and I

I first met Dr. Martin Luther King, Jr., in Montgomery, Alabama, in 1954. He had just assumed the pastorate of the Dexter Avenue Baptist Church. Dr. King and Dr. Abernathy visited my tent meeting one evening, and we engaged in a friendly, though lively, theological debate. My tent was pitched on the corner of Smythe and High Street, across from the Tijuana Night Club. Because of its location, nine hundred to eleven hundred people attended nightly. Over four hundred and fifty baptisms resulted from these efforts.

A delegation of concerned citizens petitioned the mayor to run me out of town. The mayor assigned two detectives to monitor the meetings.

"He's doing nothing but preaching the gospel," they reported back.

"You will just have to preach him out of town," the mayor informed the delegation. That couldn't happen, so I stayed until the congregation was housed in a new church building. Dr. King went on to become the dominant force in the Civil Rights movement. His primary contribution to the life of the nation is that he was used of God to force the nation to acknowledge its sin and begin to seriously reform itself. He did not claim to have done this alone. But then, therein lay his genius, the ability to get people to work together.

I was there in 1957 at the Lincoln Memorial when he delivered his famous "Give us the Ballot" speech and at many other rallies, in spite of my appointments and responsibilities at the World Headquarters of the Seventh-day Adventist Church. I was elected to this level of church government in 1954. Since then, world travel has been my venue. In spite of my traveling responsibilities, I refused to sleep through the revolution.

King never forgot me either. He and a Baptist pastor from Baltimore were riding in Washington when they saw my name on the Marquee at the famed Capital Arena. I was holding an evangelistic campaign there. "Park the car," Dr. King told the pastor. "Let's go in here and hear a good sermon." They came in and stayed the entire service. How did I get the story? The Baptist preacher with whom King was riding had a niece, Carolyn Hinson, whom I had baptized years earlier. He flew into Atlanta to Dr. King's funeral and called Carolyn to come to the airport to pick him up. While he was eating a breakfast of grits, eggs, and vegetarian stripples, he suddenly laughed. "Where is evangelist Cleveland?" he asked.

"He's headquartered in Washington," Carolyn said. He then told her the story. Neither King nor his associates knew half the people who worked at the street level to help their plans succeed. After King's death, I was a member of the Washington committee to plan the Washington phase of the poor peoples' march. In fact, I was asked to superintend feeding the hundreds of campers. The Jewish chairwoman knew of Adventists' great record in this area, but then I told her that I traveled so much that the people would probably starve to death with an "absentee feeder." I did, however, secure $15,000 from the General Conference to provide blankets and beds for the campers. We also secured an eighteen-wheeler clothing depot for Resurrection City residents. I worked with Charles Dudley and Earl Moore to assist with the medical-dental van that was the only medical facility in Resurrection City. Night after night I stayed with them helping people. I was there when the park police cleared the mall and arrested Dr. Abernathy and a few campers. Elder W. W. Fordham and I arranged to clear the warehouses of leftover food and sent three tractor-trailers full to Marks, Mississippi, for distribution to the poor. The Seventh-day Adventist Church paid the bill. The Southern Christian Leadership Conference had more help than they will ever know.

I was at Andrews University for a week of religious emphasis when Dr. King was shot. Fires were lighted across the nation. Washington, D.C., was ablaze. I flew into Washington and contacted Brother John Trusty. There were food shortages all over the city. People with money could not buy food. Brother Trusty and I turned the First Church of Seventh-day Adventists into a food distribution center. Volunteers, under Brother Trusty's direction, fed scores of people throughout the crisis.

Once I was standing at a street corner, dressed in my Adventist Community Services uniform, when a sniper opened fire a few yards away. A National Guardsman ordered me off the corner on the double as they pressed the search for the sniper. These were dangerous times.

The Northwest Airlines crew that flew me into Washington from Cleveland, Ohio, did not want to make the flight. After all, I was the only passenger.

"Washington is on fire two blocks from my house," I told them. "Prepare to fly." When we landed at Washington National Airport, I was informed that no one was allowed to enter the city. "Bed down where you are," we were told.

"But I'm a minister. I've got to get in," I replied.

"If you're a preacher, we need you in there. Go on in—if you can find a taxi that will take you," was the answer. I did. A White brother took me into Maryland, then traveled west into the District of Columbia.

My contact with Justice Thurgood Marshal was for me a source of great pride. I had heard of this great barrister and the dangerous trips into the south. His evasion of the Klan, subsequent court appearances, and his victories as a lawyer for the National Association for the Advancement of Colored People are legend. I had pitched my tent next to the University in Dar es Salaam, East Africa, when the great man was visiting there. It was Thurgood Marshall who wrote the constitutions for Kenya, Ghana, and other African nations that freed themselves from their European masters. He is still viewed as the constitutional father of those nations. Since his visit was a grand occasion, I took my congregation next door to his lecture. He spotted me standing in the crowd and sent a young man to escort me to the front. We shook hands, and he had me stand next to him during the lecture and question-and-answer period. That was as close as I got to the great man to whom we owe so much.

At my noon staff meeting in Dar, an African in a long white robe and staff in hand strode purposely toward my tent. I rose to greet him.

"Are you in charge?" he asked me.

"Yes."

"I will speak here tonight. I am a prophet," he answered.

"I am not a prophet," I answered, "but I will preach here tonight."

"Oh, you don't believe in me? I'll say this to you. Your president will die of an assassin's bullet," he predicted. We paid little attention to him then. It was September 1963. We did remember him later when, as November 22, 1963, in the same year of the prediction, president John F. Kennedy was assassinated.

John F. Kennedy offered great hope to young Africans during this period. It was the year of the struggle for the brightest minds, a peaceful tug-o'-war between the United States and Russia to educate young Africans in the ways of east and west. Each nation would airlift these young students to their respective countries and provide them scholarships. Dar es Salaam was the staging area. Scores of these young students were there, waiting to be airlifted. When I pitched my tent next to the university, many of these students, with nothing else to do, came to my meetings. Of the

112 people baptized, thirteen of them were from this student group. Eight of them chose to come to the U.S. One of them went to Poland and later became a prominent physician in Zambia. The others went to the Soviet Union.

Sinjilla, of Zambia, was one of these. He had been a strong supporter of Kenneth Kiunda, president of Zambia, who successfully contested British rule and won. Imprisoned with Kiunda for political activism by the British, he was now free to pursue his education. From the start of the meetings in Dar es Salaam, he was a thoughtful man and highly inquisitive. His plane from Russia due any day, he asked me to pray that it would not come until we completed the lectures. For four weeks, no plane came from Russia. He was converted to Christ and the teachings of the church, resolving to be baptized. Then he received word that the Soviet plane would arrive in twenty-four hours. This was two weeks before our first scheduled baptism. We took this brother to the banks of the Indian Ocean for a private baptism. I prayed that God would keep him faithful, immersed him in water in the name of the triune God, and sent him on his way.

I later learned that he refused to work on the Sabbath or to go to school on that day. After much deliberation, Soviet educational authorities gave their permission, and he successfully completed his course in economics; his relationship with Christ matured in the process. He returned to Zambia a committed Seventh-day Adventist Christian and became a highly successful businessman and elder in the Seventh-day Adventist Church. My tent in Tanzania was not only a "cold war" focal point between the world-war superpowers, but in a real sense, a battleground of cosmic forces.

8

Panther Permit

It was my habit to attend and participate in seven camp meetings per year, often doing heavy duty in each. Afterward I would visit with one of my two brothers. I was in the pulpit in New Orleans when I felt a sharp pain in the abdomen. Thinking nothing of it, I preached that morning and headed for the airport the next day. By this time, my inflamed abdomen shrieked with pain. I landed at Dulles International Airport a very sick man. I asked my wife for a laxative, blaming camp-meeting food for my malady. Instead, she called Dr. Carl Dent of the Riverside Hospital in Nashville, Tennessee. With some urgency, I was put on a plane and rushed to Nashville. Elder Norman Simons met me at the airport, and I was rushed to the doctor's busy office.

"You will need immediate surgery," I was told within minutes.

Only afterward did I learn what a close brush with death

I had. My appendix had ruptured five days earlier and, but for a miracle, I was headed for an appointment with the grim reaper. Peritonitis had infected my intestines and bladder, and there was some question if either would be functional if I survived. The call to prayer went across the nation. After praying over me, the skilled doctor did his job. My wife and son flew to my bedside. Hundreds of churches prayed for divine healing.

"When will the doctor operate?" I asked the nurse when I awoke.

"It's all over, Elder Cleveland. You're in recovery." It was a close call. A nurse told me later that he had held my intestines in his hands while the doctor bathed them in penicillin. That is all that they could do beyond praying. Would I have to wear a plastic bag to handle my waste? We could only wait for the answer. It was not long in coming. I learned that so simple a thing as a bowel movement would be the occasion of great joy. It was a sign that Jehovah's use of me would be limited only by my willingness to serve. That would prove to be unlimited.

While I was on my sickbed, the largest tent that I would ever use was being pitched in Los Angeles, California. Nobody believed that I would die then, including me. The West-Coast preachers kept in touch with Dr. Dent daily as they readied the camp for an opening date, one month after my operation. Prayers were being answered, and my recovery was steady. Opening night found me in the pulpit as expected, preaching the Word of God. My incision drained as the meetings progressed over the next ten weeks. Adhesions were so

Panther Permit · 51

severe that I had to stand on one foot during the sermons to find relief. But, sustained by God's grace, I preached six nights a week and twice on the Sabbath day. I will never forget the integrated band of workers who stood by my side. Night after night the big tent filled and often overflowed. We had to pitch an additional tent to accommodate the overflow on Sabbaths. Nearly five hundred people were baptized in that meeting.

A few hundred miles north in Oakland, California, we held a soul-winning campaign in the Oakland Alameda auditorium. The situation was unique because the Black Panther Party controlled much of life in large sections of Oakland. To operate the program, I needed a permit from Oakland and from the Black Panther Party. I sent young Walter Horton, because he was a weight lifter. Huey Newton was in jail at the time, and Bobby Seale was running the party.

Horton arrived at the party headquarters while the panther musclemen were staging their weight-lifting exercises. Spectators were standing around in awe of bulging biceps and sweat-soaked bodies. "May I join you?" he asked, smiling.

"Sure, go ahead," they said. Horton ripped off his shirt, flexed his muscles, and proceeded to out-lift the best of them.

"Come inside and meet our leader," someone said, impressed. With that, he was ushered into a chat with Bobby. Horton informed him that he was my emissary to secure his approval of our meeting to begin shortly in the civic center. Bobby said that he would send a panther to observe the opening and give his answer the following Monday. He kept his word. On Sunday, the day of my opening, his man checked in with Horton, was given a tour of the medical-dental van, and treated to an inside view of the "feed-the-hungry program." He listened intently to the sermon. The next day Horton returned to Panther headquarters for an answer. The answer was not only an approval of the program, but Horton was given a black beret, an honorary membership in the Black Panther Party. Our meetings were successful. It was an integrated endeavor, with nearly three hundred baptisms.

The Panther episode paid off in Detroit. Our meeting in this city was in the Ford Auditorium, another integrated effort. Thousands attended nightly with over three hundred baptisms. In connection with the effort, a food-distribution program was conducted from the Gratiot Center. The showpiece, though, was the giant eighteen-wheeler medical-dental van brought in from the Southwest Union Conference. We planned to park and use it in the neediest section of Detroit, offering health services there. Protection for the van and medical personnel was a problem, however. We made contact with Panther headquarters in Detroit. They sent two representatives to our planning sessions. I began by introducing myself to them.

"We know you from Oakland," they interrupted. "What can we do to help you?"

"Where can we park the van and receive protection for both property and personnel?" The next day they returned with the neighborhood designation and promises of protection. Medical and dental personnel served the neighborhood without incident for eight weeks. Neither persons nor property were harmed as the Panthers stood guard.

An interesting incident occurred on the first day. Three Caucasian nurses and one dentist were on duty at the van. They were offering pro bono services for the poor. One of the giant Panther guards stepped to the head of the line and insisted that he be treated first. He and the dentist chatted amicably for a few minutes.

"When are you going to pull my tooth?" the Panther finally asked. The dentist handed him his tooth and apologized for not informing him that it had been pulled while carrying on their conversation. This brother advertised the dentist far and wide.

"He's a painless man, painless." The treatment of mankind's ills and the supply of his needs make the preaching of the gospel effective.

This program was especially effective in New Orleans, Louisiana. In my nightly meetings, we announced that we would feed the hungry. "Just leave your name and address, and we will supply you with food," we proclaimed.

A woman from the Desire projects, a low-income area, left her name and address. The next day I decided to deliver her food. Now, my brother who pastored there had warned me not to venture down there. Believing in the power of God to protect His own, I loaded up the food and headed for the projects. When I stopped and got out of the car to inquire of the location, I was immediately surrounded by about fifteen youths. I firmly announced my name, profession, and purpose for being there. Pulling out the card, I read the woman's name who had requested the food.

54 · Let the Church Roll On

"That's my aunt!" exclaimed one of the young men. "Follow me." I had them carry the food as we followed the nephew to his aunt's house. We ascended the stairs to the apartment where she lived. Her delight in seeing us was matched only by her hunger. After prayer, the multitude fell upon the food. I left them, cooking. I only hope the aunt got some. I only got afraid after telling my experience to my brother and hearing from his lips the danger I had escaped. We baptized some jewels out of places like this. Truly, God is no respecter of persons.

9

Instrument of Change

My interest in human relations and racial matters goes back to my childhood. Because my father belonged to the Negro Voters League, he would carry me with him to the meetings, and I was introduced to "freedom" rhetoric. As early as 1942, I refused to segregate my public meetings. Large numbers of White people have always attended my meetings. Even in the deep South they had to sit where they could.

In 1943, I attended my first workers' meeting in Charlotte, North Carolina. All the White preachers sat on one side of the church, and the Black brothers sat on the other. When reporting time came, only White preachers reported. When I returned home, my wife detected my frustration. I told her of the situation and told her of my determination to "sit where I please and speak when I feel like it." The next workers' meeting, I sat on the White side. When reporting time came, I stood up and spoke my piece. The sky did not cave in, but the shock was obvious.

Some Black preachers tried to "look me down," and some White preachers tried to "stare me down." I gathered my inspiration from their shock and spoke louder and longer. After all, I had a lot to say. God had been good to us. Why shouldn't I testify? I had just completed a twelve-week evangelistic campaign. Over eighty-four people had been baptized into the church. I had a thriving radio program going, with 300 Bible-school enrollees. People were packed in the church like sardines three nights a week and on the Sabbath. I had something to say and said it. When I sat down, you could hear a pin drop. At that moment, there was change. Workers' meetings in Charlotte would never be the same.

F. O. Sanders, president of the conference, rose, solemnly surveyed the assembled preachers, then smiled. "Brother Cleveland, I commend you for this good report," he said. "I have heard your radio broadcasts. They are a credit to the church. Brother treasurer, send Brother Cleveland fifteen dollars a month for as long as he is 'on the air.' I have also monitored your tent meeting and church attendance. It is true as you say. Keep up the good work." The "die was cast." From now on, I would be a catalyst for change.

In 1950, I was the first Black man to teach White men in the history of the denomination. The Southern Union Evangelism Council was held in Panama City, Florida, when Elder V. G. Anderson designated me a principle instructor. For three days, I discussed the dynamics and methodology of evangelism to an attentive audience of more than five hundred preachers. I couldn't know then that from these beginnings I would soon preach on six continents. God's plan would unfold with time.

Since 1950, I have been in the caucus of Black executives planning change in Black-White relations. Kibble, Fordham, Wagner, Lee, Cheatham, Frank Bland, L. H. Bland, Murphy, and Singleton invited me into their inner councils. There has always been a civil rights movement going on in our church, and early on, I was a part of it. Though there was a ten-year age difference between me and my seniors, I was included.

For years there was no Black officer at the General Conference level of the church. Two laymen, Mylas Martin and Frank Hale, took on this issue—negotiating internally at first, but without success. They soon mounted a public protest, ending in demonstrations, at the General Conference sessions. Mylas Martin did not want this public display and labored long and hard to get the church leadership to change itself. I know, for we were in constant communication until the decision was made. My position was, and is, that Black preachers can and should fight for and achieve change at administrative levels and not let self-interest dictate silence on vital issues. Laymen shouldn't have to do it. Mylas was still not sure that they would demonstrate, until he went to Andrews University. There, a high church official told him to do his worst, that the General Conference was ready for any contingency. That did it.

The layman's conference would bring the leadership of the General Conference to the altar. When it was all over, there would be a Black officer in the General Conference—

with others to follow. The full force of the lay campaign hit during the General Conference session in San Francisco. Daily headlines highlighted the campaign, and *Time* magazine spread the word. Parallel sessions, orchestrated by Dr. Frank Hale, drew attention from the main sessions. Mylas Martin approached me and suggested that the time had come to call off the marches. He asked me to get the Black presidents together. After ascertaining from them that the time for cessation had come, Mylas and Dr. Hale called it off. They had cracked the wall of executive exclusion. We will ever owe them a debt of gratitude for this. The Black presidents picked me to meet the press.

From 1950, I have been a vocal part of every effort to change the racial climate in the church. There is a "paper trail" to verify it. I was a member of the first Human Rights Committee of the General Conference. Indeed, I helped set it up. I was a member of the flying squad, a committee of five, set up to investigate injustice anywhere in North America, with power to act. Elder Neal Wilson stood behind us in the decision-making process. In fact, he was helpful in the whole desegregation process. The Human Rights Committee enjoyed his fullest support. Under Elder Robert Pierson and Elder Neal Wilson, the Seventh-day Adventist Church desegregated every institution under its jurisdiction. I was an active part of that process.

In 1969, I wrote *The Middle Wall*. It was published by the Review and Herald. It is the first book about racial matters published by the church since Mrs. White wrote the *Testimonies*. The manuscript was so frank that the book editor of the Review suggested that it would have to be cleared by the panel of top executives. It was submitted to the presidential groups.

"Publish it yesterday," Elder Neal Wilson said.

I still don't understand how this man became president of a conservative church organization, considering the many liberal causes he championed. It must have been God's will. Some of the Blacks gave him plenty of leverage with which to pressure his reluctant White colleagues. Elder Pierson suggested that I add to one chapter, and he would OK it. With these two endorsements, he gave the order to publish. Later on, I submitted *Free at Last*. It was published, and though banned in old South Africa, it still enjoys healthy sales across the Black world.

When I entered the General Conference, there was only one Black secretary in the building, Mrs. Evelyn Mays Johnson. I decided to challenge the system on a most sensitive issue. I would be the first Black man to have a White secretary in the history of the church. In time, this would in turn lead to Black secretaries serving White leaders. It was easy to get it done. First, I visited Evelyn Mays Johnson and explained my plan to her. I told her that she would get a phone call that day asking her to be my secretary. She already worked for Elders Peterson and Moseley, both Black. I told her to inform the caller that she was too busy working for two bosses already. She did this and "the fat was in the fire." That day, the decision was made, and a young British housewife volunteered to be my secretary. The experiment was so successful that, as Blacks were elected, they were given White secretaries. We had to call a meeting and call for a reversal of policy so that more Black secretaries could be hired, the idea in the first place. Another barrier had fallen.

As the first Black man to integrate a department of the General Conference, the problem was simple. "Act or be acted upon." Since I would be in close association with Whites who knew little about Blacks, it would be my solemn duty to educate them to live around "nonpassive" Blacks, which I am.

Two stories will illustrate the point. During one of my visits abroad, we stopped with a family that had been overseas for many years.

"Brother Cleveland, we are giving you our own bed to sleep in," the wife of the White missionary announced after greeting us. "And for dinner we have a treat for you. We have black-eyed peas, persimmons, and watermelon." I excused myself. Entering the restroom, I couldn't contain my hearty laugh.

"What do you feed your husband?" I asked, returning. "I'll eat that. I don't like black-eyed peas, and persimmons aren't my favorite. As for watermelon, just feed me what you feed your husband." She was properly educated. I was heartbroken for having to sacrifice that watermelon to the cause of education.

The other story is equally illustrative. I landed in the Philippines as the first Black sent to the country by my church. I was met at the airport by an official delegation of my White brethren. As we drove through the beautiful streets of Manila, one of them told a Negro joke. Everybody laughed but me. The atmosphere changed as I began to ask about the monuments that we were passing. After we were comfortably settled, one of the brethren was not sure that he could work with me for the period of our joint assignment.

"What is the problem?" I asked.

"You're hypersensitive," he answered.

"What makes you think that?"

"The joke, you didn't laugh at the joke," he answered.

"Well, I didn't think it was funny," I replied.

"Well, what was wrong with it?" he asked.

"Well, brother," I replied, "we Black folk have hundreds of White folk jokes that we tell among ourselves. We've been laughing at you folk for 200 years. But we respect you too much to tell them to you. We expect the same respect."

"All right, tell me one, and I will understand." I told him one. He laughed for five full minutes. I thought he would burst a blood vessel. "All right," he said when he pulled himself together, "I understand. I will spread the word ahead of you—no Negro jokes." He kept his word.

Entering old South Africa was some experience. Big signs reading "White" and "Non-White" guarded each entrance at the airport. I sent my wife and son through the "Non-White" entrance. I entered the land of apartheid under the White sign, just testing. A representative of the Adventist Union office met me and took us by car to the Union office. He warned me that two CID officers were waiting to interrogate me and hoped I would not make a mistake and say something wrong. I suggested with equal vocal intensity that if he didn't relax, he would make me nervous. If so, I would

62 · Let the Church Roll On

make mistakes that South Africa would never forget. Much to my relief, he quieted down.

We arrived at the office, and, sure enough, the federal officers were there. After proper greetings, the feds took over. They turned on the recorder and the questioning began.

"What do you think of our government?" they asked.

"I just entered the country," I answered. "How could I be expected to form an intelligent opinion in so short a time? Your government criticized Shirer for his opinion of you based on a two-week trip through your country. I have been here two hours, and you ask for an opinion. Why not ask my wife? She spent seven years of her life down here." Shocked, they turned their full attention to her. She charmed them by speaking Afrikaans, complimenting the geography and the people. These men, though trained in the art of suspicion, gave us their blessing and left. The church authorities were relieved, temporarily.

One week into my visit, I preached to an integrated audience at City Hall in Cape Town. "We have learned to fly the air like birds, swim the sea like fish. When will we learn to walk the earth like brothers?" I said. On Monday morning, one CID officer was waiting for me.

"Well, what do you think of us now?" he asked.

"My church has kept me too busy to study civics," I replied.

"What do you think of Martin Luther King?" he asked.

"The 22 million Negroes in America view him as a great man and an effective leader," I replied.

"Would you lead a protest against the laws of your

Instrument of Change · 63

government?" he asked.

"My church believes in the separation of church and state," I answered, "therefore we object to the state dictating to the church." Satisfied, he detached the tape recorder and left. I was relieved that he had not asked the real question; namely, would you march against the laws of your government as an individual? My answer to that question would have gotten me kicked out of the country.

For, you see, I have marched against legal injustice with other concerned citizens. But I did so, not as a representative of my church, but as an individual citizen exercising my civil rights.

I was part of the movement to organize Black Seventh-day Adventist conferences into two union conference organizational units. This would have channeled more Black-contributed finance into projects directly affecting Black people. Since all the regional Black conferences are open to all races and indeed are multiracial, this is not segregation; but because they cover large Black neighborhoods, they are managed by Black officers. Most people forget that while Martin Luther King championed integration, he pastored a Black church. A measure of self-determination must accompany integration, or it will ever lead to minority frustration.

Another problem was that the union presidency was all White for over ninety years. The Black union plan would have put two Black presidents on the controlling panel. We were defeated. Elder Wilson, however, realized that something must be done. He helped one existing union entity to elect a Black Union president. Elder Robert Carter has capably filled that post for three terms. The problem is that the change is not systematic, and, therefore, when he retires, it will revert. Voting with a White majority guarantees this. David Taylor, another Black, has been elected president of the Atlantic Union. We applaud this action. But without quota system by policy, time never favors a minority.

In Oakland, California, a friend of mine handed me a piece of paper. "Read it," he said. "I think you will know what to do with it." It was Ellen White's will. It was, and remains, on file in the Oakland-Alameda courthouse. The will provides that a percentage of the royalties from all her published writings be donated to the Black work. I traveled across the country with this "bombshell" in my pocket trying to decide the best possible use to be made of the information. I called C. E. Dudley for counsel. We decided that it must be shared with the Black presidents.

From that meeting came the decision to have a formal meeting with Elder Neal Wilson concerning the matter. We presented the will to him. Surprised at its contents, he agreed to have the chairman of the E. G. White Estate explain the "will situation." The next day, Arthur White was given thirty minutes of time to explain to the assembled delegates from all over the world that the prophet's will was a "dry will." The members of the family had not received a thing, he explained. All the profits had been recycled into the "in-house" operation, he said.

We listened attentively, knowing that this could not, and would not, be the end of the matter. Having "disposed" of the prophet's will, Elder Wilson proposed the "Regional Reversion Fund," a special financial allocation to Black conferences that would rotate among the conferences at the rate of two conference beneficiaries per year. For the first time in my life, I was put on the finance committee of the Annual Administrative Council. I questioned the wisdom of the appointment until I saw the agenda. Elder Frank Bland and I were the only two Blacks in the room. Elder Wilson had done his part. The Regional Reversion Fund was on the committee agenda. The debate was on. White conservatives were beating the plan to death.

"Don't give them special consideration. No affirmative action. Let them stand on their own feet," were some of the arguments. Elder Bland was heartsore as he made an impassioned appeal for the financial measure. They listened respectfully and began again to filibuster the plan to death. In the closing moments of the debate, with the cause virtually lost, I took the floor. My speech was short.

"My brethren, I have sat in silent shock listening to your speeches. I have never been in a finance committee session and will probably never attend another. I arise to confess to a grave mistake. You see, I have held the opinion that you men were like Elder Wilson. We deal with him every day and find him sensitive to minority special needs and concerns. He does not always agree with us, but he does understand what we are talking about. I naively assumed that you were like him. It saddens me to learn that I am mistaken."

With that I sat down. There was a moment of deep silence in that room. Then one by one, the opponents of the allocation stood and affirmed their support for the measure, and the Regional Reversion Fund became law. Brother Wilson smiled, I slipped out of the building into the sunlight, and the church rolled on.

10

Modern Miracle

In 1966 the church sent me to Port-of-Spain, Trinidad, to conduct a field school of evangelism. Dr. Eric Williams was the nation's president, and his government encouraged all religions. Forty-eight ministers and Bible instructors were flown in from thirteen countries to participate and receive training. S. L. Gadsby was the host president, and Roy Hoyte, a capable member of the Caribbean Union Conference, was the coordinator. As the workers gathered, little indicated that the largest influx of souls since Pentecost was about to occur. This was far from my thinking as I flew south. My plane landed in the darkness at Piarco Airport.

The preachers pitched two large tents near the Savannah, expecting about two thousand people per night. There is a large East Indian population there, mostly Hindu. The Roman Catholic and Anglican Churches are very strong. To my consternation, I found that I had landed in the Caribbean during the rainy season. To add to our woes, there was no history of fruitful evangelism in Trinidad. A White evangelist had baptized just sixty-four people in a campaign amidst great rejoicing. It was tough territory.

From the beginning, our prayers were answered. Seven thousand to eight thousand people per night crowded the grounds to hear the Word of God, each night a Pentecostal experience. The preachers visited homes.

"No buildings were shaken, but lives were," someone wrote. The nightly response startled us. People traveled over sixty miles nightly to hear the Word. The meetings were under-funded but over-endowed. To the steady sound of falling rain, we prayed for the "latter rain." Our prayers were answered. Over eight hundred and twenty-four people were baptized and 220 decisions were made on the closing night. I could not get a visa extension, so evangelist G. H. Rainey was called in to follow up the meetings. Over four hundred more were added to the faith.

From the beginning, the weather in the tropical rainy season was a problem. We preachers met daily to pray for good weather during our meetings each night at seven o'clock. God answered our prayers. Not a meeting was rained on for eight weeks. It would rain all day until 5:00 p.m. Then the sun would shine brightly and dry things up. One hour after the meetings closed, rain poured again. For eight weeks this continued. The miracle was so obvious that others noticed the phenomena. A few years later, I returned to Port-of-Spain for a visit. The cab drivers remembered me.

"Here comes the man who stopped the rain," one shouted.

Modern Miracle · 69

"You're mistaken," I told him, "but I know the One who did."

The victories were real and lasting. One man who had resisted Adventism for thirty-five years, though married to an Adventist wife, was baptized midst shouts of praise. One ministerial visitation team brought 101 people for baptism. We had three levels of instruction for the candidates. There were the nightly services, house visitation, and a baptismal review. When over six hundred people showed up with their baptismal clothing for baptism, a church official wanted to know if the church board had processed each name. "Brother," I told him, "the church manual was not written for Pentecost. Get busy and help me interrogate those people." He fell into line, and the church rolled on.

Upon my return to Washington, I was asked about this "infraction" of the church rules.

I told the questioner, "Imagine! Four church boards trying to evaluate the religious experiences of over eight hundred people. We had the whole congregation vote the saints in on the profession of their faith and proceeded with the baptism. Events were moving too swiftly for ecclesiastical deliberation."

Thousands of people lined the banks of the river as the baptism commenced.

The Cathedral Quartet, composed of Benjamin Reaves, James Edgecombe, Elbert Shepperd, and William Scales, provided music. Forty preachers went into the water to perform the rites. The people were baptized twenty at a time. It took four and a half hours to baptize them all. The sun was setting when the last saint was immersed. Jehovah had made history in this island nation. The denomination built a new church on a nearby hill. The members named it Cleveland Temple.

The meetings impacted the world church. A preacher from Spain came to the Caribbean and baptized over fifteen hundred people in one campaign. He told me that his vision lifted when he saw the Trinidad effort. If you examine the statistics of the Inter-American Division before 1966 and after, you will understand Eric John Murray's characterization of the Trinidad campaign as pivotal in the division's surge in memberships. J. C. Palmer returned to Jamaica and baptized over four hundred souls. Valentine returned to Santo Domingo and baptized over five hundred. What Trinidad did was increase the expectancy level of the individual evangelist. From the General Conference level, we promoted the "Men of the Century" program to feed the fever. The spirit of Trinidad affected the world.

I visited Costa Rica and conducted a seven-day workshop in evangelism, with emphasis on expectations. At the end of the week, I asked the men to set a goal for next year's baptisms. They came in with a modest increase over the previous year's achievement. No one was more surprised than I at what happened next.

I leapt to my feet, grabbed the poster of "modest goals," flung it to the floor, and stomped on it. Everyone gaped in shock. I heard myself chastening them for their unbelief, urging them to greater efforts and expectations. It was all so spontaneous, so sudden. A stunned silence followed. I knew that I must have worn out my welcome. The "committee on goals" slipped quietly out of the room. I assumed they were preparing to escort me to the airport, so I began conditioning my mind for the persona nongrata soon to follow. Instead, they returned with smiles on their faces. They thanked me for my emotional demonstration. They confessed that they needed it. They unfolded a new banner on which they proposed to baptize twice the number of the previous year. God was surely with me. My cup runneth over.

One year later at an official gathering, a church official embraced me and joyfully announced that they had exceeded their goal and thanked me for the "explosion." Personally, I can assume no credit for even a fraction of the evangelistic explosion that has made Adventist history. To be used of God in any small way has been my highest privilege. After Port-of-Spain, 1966, expectations and results skyrocketed.

11

Washington

Elected to the World Conference of the church in 1954, I had an immediate problem. My department head informed me that my public evangelistic career was now over and that, henceforth, I would teach others how to do it. I explained to him that the best way to teach evangelism was to do it and that I would be leaving San Francisco for Montgomery, Alabama, to begin a major campaign within the month. I added that there would be thirteen young ministers there getting "on-the-job-training."

"Perhaps," I said to him, "you should get another man."

R. A. Anderson smiled understandingly and prayed for me. "I'll see you in Washington after Montgomery," he said. He did better than that. He visited me in Montgomery.

Upon our arrival in Washington, the beauty of the place struck us. Only Paris rivals Washington for natural beauty. We were to live there from 1954 to 1977, twenty-three eventful years. During this period, I would visit sixty-seven countries, preach on six continents, and author fourteen published books and two Sabbath School quarterlies. I would coordinate evangelism of the North American Division, 1972-1977, serve as associate editor of the *Ministry* magazine, and be a columnist for the *Regional Voice*. I would author a devotional book of the year, train over sixteen hundred ministers worldwide, and serve as visiting professor at Oakwood College for twenty-six years and Andrews University for twenty-three years.

I also received the D.D. degree from Andrews University and the L.L.D. degree from Daniel Payne College, was inducted into the Martin Luther King, Jr., Preachers Hall of Fame at Morehouse College in Atlanta, Georgia, and was the subject of Dr. E. E. Rogers's doctoral thesis at Michigan State University and also the subject of Don Jacobson's master's degree thesis at Andrews University. I would be cited in *Who's Who in Black America* and in *Who's Who in Religion in America*. The governor of the state of Alabama would designate me Alabama's Most Distinguished Black Clergyman on March 8, 1989. I would be elected "alumnus of the year" at Oakwood College twice. I would be the first Black man sent by the General Conference to Asia, Europe, and Australia. It was a busy life indeed.

Some have speculated widely on how I could spend twenty-three years as an associate secretary of the Ministerial Association without promotion to "higher office." Calvin Rock, in his doctoral thesis, wrote that there must have been some disappointment. Those who know me best, know better. In all my professional career, I have had little interest in anything but evangelism. This accounts for my "freedom of expression" in matters of race. My stand on racial matters has often brought me into conflict with the "powers that be." But this has not silenced my pen or voice. Dr. Rock's puzzlement in his thesis is due to the fact that he was still in school while I was busy with my brethren making the "rough places plain, and crooked places straight." It was this good man who provided me a situation of dignity when I left the General Conference.

In all fairness to church administrators, you should know that they tried to promote me twice. When Elder Frank Bland retired, he came by my office. "I have recommended you to succeed me as the Black vice president of the General Conference," he said.

"What?"

"The brethren have accepted my recommendation," he added. "So don't turn it down."

I sat there thinking about the possibilities.

Later that same day, Bob Spangler dropped by for a visit and casually said, "They're moving you to officers' row." When I expressed some doubt, he told me of corroboration that was on the way. At 4:00 p.m., Elder Pierson's secretary phoned. She told me "You are to meet at the president's apartment at 6:30 p.m. for a 'chat and chew.' " I headed home in a state of shock. I would become the highest-ranking Black man in the denomination. No!

I didn't want it.

How would I derail this? I thought. The promotion was

on the way. If I could smile my way through the "chat and chew," I would go down in history as the third Black vice president of the General Conference. But administrative duties were not for me. I told my wife of my dilemma. She understood. "How are you going to get out of it?" she asked.

"I will need your help. At the 'chat and chew,' the White officers will talk about many sensitive subjects. I will nudge you when the appropriate moment comes."

At half past six, at the president's apartment, all the assembled brass were present. It was my final screening. The conversation moved easily from one sensitive topic to another. Finally, someone mentioned Richard Nixon. Praise flowed in all directions of the president's performance. I nudged my wife.

"Well," she said, "Tricky Dick is not as popular in our neighborhood as he is in yours." The room froze. It was like the "night before Christmas." Then, all eyes turned toward me.

"That's right," I said. "I voted against him the last time. I can hardly wait to send him into retirement at the next election." For the next twenty minutes, conversation was difficult, and digestion more so. This effectively terminated my upward mobility. In Mexico City, however, where the election would take place, the nominating committee was in the process of electing me anyhow. Those were men from all over the world. For twenty minutes my name was the only one on the board. Speeches were being made in my favor. The process was well under way when the president of the General Conference entered, apologized for being late, and proceeded to read a list of names of men that "he could live comfortably with." My name was not on the list. Another was elected. I breathed a sign of relief. I had been saved by a "chat and chew." Whew! Blame no one else. I was the architect of the "Passover."

It would happen once more. My dear wife, who has sustained my ministry wholeheartedly, was overtaken in 1971 by an arthritic condition that grew progressively worse. I reached the point that travel on a worldwide scale had to be curtailed. I made the decision to leave the General Conference so that I could take better care of her. She protested the decision but relented when I reminded her that she had given her life in service to her Lord and me and that neither He nor I would neglect her now. I had just been reelected to the Ministerial Association for four more years and had served one of the four when I made the decision to leave in 1977. The president of the General Conference remonstrated with me for forty minutes, urging me to reconsider.

"I could move you down here with me," the good man said.

"What specifically do you mean?" I asked.

"We would make you an officer of the General Conference, and you could travel at your own discretion," he replied.

"But, Mr. President, I don't want *up*; I want *out*," I answered. This ended my second shot at administrative glory. When I left, they wanted me to stay. I had three more years of my term left. My departure in 1977 was of my own free will and volition. Evangelism is my passion, my "long suit."

I love and respect administrators but have absolutely no desire to be one. Indeed, when H. D. Singleton moved to New York as president of the Northeastern Conference, the committee that elected his replacement offered the presidency of the South Atlantic to me. I was in a tent meeting in Charleston, South Carolina, when a delegation arrived. They sat patiently through the services and followed me to my trailer, where my wife served them hot drinks and cookies for three hours while I said No to their generous proposal to be their president. The ability to sit for hours making policy and transacting business is a God-given gift. Jehovah bypassed me when dishing it out. Standing in a pulpit with a message from God, with words inspired by a higher power changing the atmosphere with the living presence—that's for me, sir, that's for me. Simply that. Nothing more.

As I mentioned, Calvin Rock was most kind to me at the time of my retirement. Here are his words, as published in the church's weekly paper, the *Adventist Review*.

On Making a Difference
Guest Editorial by
Calvin B. Rock, General Conference Vice President

"We have no great men among us" (*Evangelism*, p. 134). The Seventh-day Adventist Church is fashioned to exalt Christ, not humanity. In our movement there is no place for a cult of personality. The peaks that give definition to our history are the triumphs of our global cause and not the glories of our individuals careers.

And yet it is undeniably true that some men and women

do make a difference. We occasionally are blessed with the ministry of those whose careers are epochal, who make an impact upon established patterns of functioning in ways that are substantive and enduring. They are the few whose labors effect the expansion of our parameters, rare leaders who have been equipped by God for special service and who, under God, have contributed so as to make no small difference among us. Individuals of recent memory such as Fordyce Detamore, H. M. S. Richards, R. A. Anderson, Anna B. Knight, and F. L. Peterson all qualify for such description—and so does E. Earl Cleveland.

Cleveland has made a difference. It is not precisely quantifiable (the alterations of history never are), but his evangelistic methods, practiced and taught in Korea, England, Brazil, Finland, Indonesia, Trinidad, Poland, South Africa, Canada, Japan, India, Australia, and numerous other countries, as well as in 35 cities of the United States, are a contribution of stellar proportions.

Cleveland has made a difference in tents, halls, auditoriums, and sanctuaries on every continent of the globe; in the pages of the 11 books he has written; in the two Sabbath School quarterlies he has authored; in the many articles he has produced for *Ministry, Message,* the *Adventist Review,* and other significant Adventist publications; in scores of workers' meetings, where he has shared his techniques with an appreciative ministry; in the environs of the General Conference, where he served for 21 years; in the classrooms of Andrews University; and at Oakwood College, where he taught religion and directed a highly successful student missionary program for the past eight years.

His retirement is an event that should not go unnoticed by the world church. His students, friends, and spiritual children throughout our world divisions would like to know that he and Celia, whose charm and talent have meant so much to his effectiveness, are formally withdrawing from full-time service and will now have much more time to enjoy each other and their Huntsville home.

Larger Than Tradition

Someday, if time lasts, a more conclusive statement regarding the life and ministry of E. Earl Cleveland will appear in the pages of the *Adventist Review*, but he will not be able to see or appreciate that. This one he can. Tributes of this kind are not given to every worker whose status changes from full-time to retiree. But then some lives are larger than tradition.

"There are no great men among us," but there have been and are luminaries whose unique gifts and sacrificial dedication have permanently altered the landscapes of our dwellings. E. Earl Cleveland is such a person. We here at the General Conference would like him to know that we recognize this, and we would like you to know that we have told him so.

12

Oh Yeah!

As I read the news of the slaughter in Rwanda, I remember vividly preaching to 21,000 people there years before. Once, during a sermon, I tested my sermon's effect.

"God can't approve drinking alcoholic beverages, can He?" I shouted.

"Oh yeah," they answered back. Nonplused but courageous, I decided to try again.

"God can't take an adulterer to heaven, can He?" I thundered.

"Oh yeah," they shouted back. I bravely finished my sermon and made it to the dinner table, feeling sick. The people weren't getting it. The missionary kept flashing an amused smile my way. Finally he spoke.

"You looked a little puzzled when the people shouted their response," he smiled. "You should know the people were in complete agreement with you."

"They were?"

"Out here 'Oh yeah' means NO!" I was relieved.

Out there, I met both the tallest people in the world, the Watusis, and the shortest, the Pygmies. I shook hands with a Pygmy chief and gave him salt. There were no Pygmy Christians in the forest when I was there. Two Christian Catholic nuns lived with this particular tribe, sharing the Pygmy way of life. It was a great sacrifice for them, being Belgian and used to modern finery. The missionaries would get the Pygmies to attend church and school. But soon their students would disappear. When found, their explanation was simple. "The forest calls me," they said.

This picture has now changed for the better. There are Pygmy pastors, educators, and church members. I shook hands with two of them at the General Conference session in New Orleans.

One day, driving along near the Ituri forest, we approached a group of about fifteen Pygmies from the rear. Pastor Muderspach stopped the car.

"Close your eyes," he told me. I did. "Open them," he said again. There was not a Pygmy in sight.

"Where did they go?" I asked. We got out and looked around, but could not find one. We got into the car and drove a short distance.

"Look behind you," the pastor said. The fifteen Pygmies were walking along, chatting happily. The Lord has compensated them for their lack of height, making them masters of camouflage.

I went on to Usambura. An interview had been scheduled with Rudahigwa, giant king of the Congo.

"We are honored to have you in our country," he said through a translator. "After reading about your president, Abraham Lincoln, I have freed all slaves in my country." I commended him for this and assured him that he would be honored in history for his act. He liked my speech and invited me to a giant celebration in the stadium. About forty thousand people gathered for the famous dance of the Watusis. About twenty Watusis appeared and began an unforgettable display of rhythmic athleticism. This world-famous dance is one of the seven wonders of the world. Each dancer is over seven feet tall. There are thousands of Africans back there who would change the rules of track and field and basketball for the world if given a chance.

One morning the missionary was in a hurry to meet an urgent appointment.

"The Watusi chief is about to confiscate our mission property in the name of the state. Cleveland, you've got to help us," he said. We dressed hurriedly, ate breakfast, and headed into the hills. After a two-hour drive, we broke into a clearing where about one hundred modern bungalows with red tile roofs lay nestled together with a tile factory nearby. I hadn't the slightest idea of what the property dispute was all about, nor what I could do about it. I suppose the missionary counted on my being Black to help. It did. We were ushered into the presence of the chief, a Roman Catholic, who greeted me warmly.

What am I supposed to do? Shouldn't I have been briefed, I wondered, *or did the missionary simply feel that the less I knew the better?* Too late now, I was deep in the action. "Welcome to my humble house," the chief said. "It is an honor to entertain one of such dignity."

"Honorable sir, chief administrator of this important territory, it is I who am privileged. You are a man of authority, dignity, and intelligence. I noticed the homes and the red tile roofs and the tile factory. Chief, America will hear about you and your progressive rule." This warmed him up. He made another speech. I made a fervent reply. He smiled and gave orders to a servant, who left hastily and returned with two mugs of buttermilk. Time for two more speeches. He toasted me, and I toasted him. We touched mugs and drank. After two farewell speeches, I made my departure.

The missionary was jubilant. *Why?* I wondered. Nothing had been said about the confiscation of property. The chief had totally ignored him. But the missionary was smiling and humming a tune.

"You saved us, Cleveland. All is well."

"How do you know?" I asked, more bewildered than ever.

"The buttermilk! The buttermilk!" he shouted. "When he ordered the buttermilk, it meant peace. No confiscation." I should have been relieved, but for the buttermilk churning inside me. I certainly did not share the patriotism of the man who said, "I only regret that I have but one life to give for the church property."

My gastric concerns were unfounded. For soon the buttermilk blended with my constitution without conflict. The church rolled on.

13

Where Shall I Go?

Most of America's inner-city population is non-White. "White flight" is a fact of life. As Blacks become more affluent, they join the exodus. The institutions in these areas reflect this demographic change. Churches, schools, economics, and politics reflect these shifts. Most major businesses follow the dollar—explaining the large suburban shopping centers. Differences are seen in government financial allocations to these Black enclaves. Under insensitive administrations, monies to the cities have been drastically cut. Our cities have been in a state of crisis for some time.

The Seventh-day Adventist Church has long maintained a program of health and welfare worldwide. But as the crisis deepened and riots exploded in major cities, Walter Fordham and I approached Elder Neal Wilson about an enlarged inner-city program for the cities. Elder Wilson convened a committee to study the matter. Elders Fordham, Bland, and

I were the Black preachers on the committee. Elder Fordham made the opening appeal, but then left to catch a plane. Elder F. L. Bland spoke in support of increased allocation of money to meet inner-city needs. In my presentation, I cited the van services of the South Central Conference, started by C. E. Dudley and Earl Moore, as an example of meeting human needs. There were people on the committee who did not see the urgency of the situation and who felt that money could be better spent "preaching the gospel." Elder Wilson ate lunch with me at the break. The verbal complaints had been severe. *How could anyone fail to see the need for this proposal?* I puzzled, frustrated.

"I'm not going to say another word. I am getting nowhere," I said.

"Why quit when you're winning?" Brother Wilson asked, a twinkle in his eye. With renewed courage, I resumed the debate. The committee approved the inner-city program for the division and engineered it into church law. Thousands of dollars were released to conferences for medical-dental services, flood distribution, and other forms of emergency relief. Now, most conferences operate the vans on a continuing basis. Some are eighteen-wheelers. Whenever there is a catastrophe—flood, earthquake, hurricane, or tornado—an Adventist is there, often ahead of the Red Cross, and always in cooperation with them.

During the Detroit riots in the wake of Martin Luther King's death, martial law was declared. Soldiers everywhere. No one was allowed in certain neighborhoods after curfew. The Lake Region Conference community services van, driven by Charles Joseph and Calvin Rock, however, was given carte blanche, instant access to the areas of greatest danger. These men were kept busy taking pregnant women to hospitals and delivering food to the needy. Some businesses were saved by the owner painting the words "Soul Brother" on the front of their stores. One evening while brethren Rock and Joseph were patrolling, a giant American tank pulled into an intersection. Someone had painted these words under the gun, "Soul-seeker." The tragedy was not without its humor.

The South Central Conference van is the most well-known of all Adventist community vehicles. It was in the march on Washington, the poor people's march, and the second Memphis march in honor of the slain civil rights leader, Martin Luther King. At a recent gathering of SCLC leadership, Earl Moore was justly honored for his humanitarian participation in these and other events. He knows that there were supportive unseen hands on the wheel of humanitarian effort. I do, too, for *I was there*.

The stress accompanying the civil rights demonstrations often confused foreign reporters. I landed on Taipei, Formosa, when the Little Rock High School was being integrated. Pictures of the confrontations were flashed around the world. Twenty-four Chinese newspeople plied me with questions.

"Is a racial uprising about to start?" one asked.

"No," I answered. "You are witnessing a new nation experiencing 'growing pains.' "

One of the largest SCLC annual celebrations occurs in Saint Petersburg, Florida. I have served as main speaker there twice. Dignitaries from the city and state always attend. I was credited by the director for helping get a boulevard named in King's honor.

My book *Free at Last* was written over a period of two and a half years. With a Negro spiritual background, I wrote it to relate the gospel of Christ to the Black experience. It hit the streets in the nick of time. Many book salesmen credit this book with saving their lives in Black neighborhoods. It is illustrated with pictures and drawings of Black achievers. Coming at a time of Black consciousness, it was an instant hit. Along with my books *Living Soul*, and *No Stranger Now*, *Free at Last* became a career and lifesaver for the door-to-door book salesperson.

One day while I sat in my office, the phone rang. It was Seville Brown, of Saint Petersburg, Florida.

"Brother Cleveland," he said, "I have just finished watching an installment of roots, and I want to ask you a question. Was Mrs. Ellen G. White a Black woman? To me it would be a source of great pride, considering her great accomplishments."

"I just don't know," I replied. He was indignant and said so emphatically. In the midst of his forceful speech, I interrupted him. "Seville, you're chicken. Why don't you write those words. Put them on paper."

"I will," he said and hung up the phone. A few days later, his letter arrived. It was hotter than the phone conversation. I took his letter, wrapped it with one of my own, and sent the inquiry to Arthur White, Ellen's grandson.

"Was Ellen G. White a Black woman?" My letter was a request for specific information. After a few weeks of silence,

I received a reply from Arthur. It was a nice letter in which he stated that it would not matter to him if she were Black. And he included an ethnic history of his great-grandfather—Mr. Harmon. Nothing on Ellen's mother. I forwarded the incomplete information to Brother Brown, who immediately phoned me. "Brother Cleveland," he shouted like a brave on the warpath, "Where's the ethnic info on Mrs. Harmon, Mrs. White's mother?"

"Write another letter," I urged him. A few days later, I received his letter requesting the missing information. I wrote a cover letter to Arthur, urging that he send me the missing biography of Mrs. Harmon so that I could satisfy the brother's thirst for knowledge and my own. Over fifteen years have passed, and this letter remains unanswered.

In the light of this experience, I believe that Ellen G. White was a Black woman, she had Black roots. Since God is no respecter of person, why not? William Foy, who received the earlier visions, was Black. As Brother Brown says, what a boost to Black morale it would be if this information were confirmed and circulated. One thing is certain, she was one of the best friends Black America has ever known.

14

The King's Palace

The year was 1955. I was on an airplane headed for Kampala, Uganda, for a ministerial training program. Being on a plane was itself a miracle, for I had solemnly promised my wife on our wedding day never to board a plane and never to live in Georgia. I broke the second vow by living in beautiful Atlanta for four of the most pleasant years of our lives. Now this—my first flight over thousands of miles of ocean—and I couldn't swim. Compounding my sense of insecurity, the copilot kept shining a flash of light on one engine. This could only be bad news. I didn't eat on the nine-hour flight because there were no vegetarian meals in those days on planes. I broke my fast with gusto in the Shannon, Ireland, airport at Pan Am's expense. The next morning I was winging my way into the heart of Africa via British overseas airlines. We landed at Entebbe Airport, the same Entebbe where a group of terrorists later held hundreds of innocent people during Idi Amin's presidency.

I landed at a slightly more peaceful time—amidst a political crisis of the first magnitude. British colonial rule was a fact of life in Uganda. There was also a structured Baganda government with a degree of autonomy. In fact, when the historian Speake first entered Uganda, he found a functioning government with the king, Kabaka, at its head and a ruling council called the Lukiko. The people wore clothes, and societal lines were drawn. Doing little to interfere with this system, the British simply imposed its controls on it. This led to inevitable conflict.

The timing of this political crisis was most unfortunate. It happened just prior to my arrival in Uganda. The king and his Lukiko objected to certain decisions of the colonial government. Colonial authorities reacted decisively to this challenge to British authority. They spirited the king out of the country. When the Baganda awakened, their king was in London, their country under martial law. Churches, businesses, and call-assembly programs were boycotted.

Into this atmosphere I arrived to hold an evangelistic field school. Twenty young Africans from four countries were brought in for the program. We would study public evangelism in the morning and hold a public meeting in the afternoon. A British preacher by the name of M. E. Lind had held successful meetings in Kampala, raising up the Naja Nacombe Church in the city. He spoke Ugandan fluently and was a close friend of the Kabaka. This would later prove valuable to me.

The British, not wanting large gatherings of people, didn't

allow me public land where I could pitch my tent. We finally found an Indian who rented us his woodyard just a stone's throw from Makkere College. This gave me access to many potential professionals. The problem: How does one get a crowd in an atmosphere of political hostility?

Some elders met with us in prayer over the problem. One of them, a member of the Lukiko, thought that if we would access the palace and impress the queen to attend the opening meeting, we would get a good crowd on opening day. He had connections in the palace and agreed to try. Our prayers were answered. We were granted an audience with the queen.

The palace itself, carpeted with plush Persian rugs, was a huge complex of modern architecture. Upon entry, we were instructed in palace protocol and sat prayerfully waiting the queen's arrival. Soon she entered, surrounded by servants who saw to her every need. She was every inch queen—resplendent in royal garb, articulate in several languages, and educated in England.

"Teacher," she said to me, "what brings you to my country?"

I made the speech of my life. So much depended on it. When I concluded my canvas, she conversed with my associates in another language for fifteen minutes. This gave me time to pray. She stood. We stood. Then came the announcement.

"Teacher, I will attend your opening service." We were ecstatic. We had to build a second platform, equal in height to the one from which I preached. Converting a sofa into a throne, we were ready for business. I placed a sign in front of the tent—"Baobula Yoyeyogerera." "Let the Bible speak for itself," it meant.

"What time should we schedule the daily meetings?" Pastor Muderspach asked.

"Eight o'clock each evening," I said.

"Then there will be nobody here," he argued. "The best time is five o'clock." I yielded to conventional wisdom, preparing for the grand opening.

The word spread. The queen would be at my opening service. The good Indian's woodyard had never known a scene like this. Hundreds of people spread all over the road and the adjoining field. Students poured down the hill from the university. Shortly after five o'clock, the black Rolls Royce of royalty, escorted by six motorcycle policemen, pulled up to the tent in a cloud of dust. All stood in respectful silence as the queen entered, assisted by Prince George Juko, brother to the king.

I prayed and promptly began my sermon: "The Handwriting on the Wall." My translator, D. K. Bazara, did a great job under difficult circumstances. He was later replaced by Mr. Kelebu, a professor of mathematics at the school of engineering. The Baganda teased me for "wearing out" two translators. The queen enjoyed the service and announced that she would return the next night. In fact, she didn't miss a night for two weeks. News reached England of her daily visits. Alarmed that she might become a Seventh-day Adventist, the archbishop of Canterbury, Geoffrey Fisher, an Anglican, warned her that if she did not cease coming, he would cease his efforts to get the king restored to his throne

The King's Palace · 95

in Uganda. What would she do? M. E. Linn visited the exiled king in London and helped resolve the dilemma.

"Stop attending the meetings," the king advised his wife. "Invite the preacher to the palace to give Bible studies." So, for the remainder of my stay in Uganda, I studied in the palace with the queen and her courtiers. Eight of the palace attendants were baptized, including George Juko, brother of the Kabaka. The queen expressed her desire to be baptized, but she was reluctant to do so while her husband was in exile.

Each day at the meetings, the C. I. D. had detectives monitor my message. I was pleased with this, hoping to get some cops converted. But they were hostile, bent on getting me out of the country. One Friday morning, I was summoned to the office of Inspector Martin, C. I. D. chief. He greeted me cordially and quickly got down to business.

"My detectives inform me that you have violated the terms of your permit to stay here any longer. What do you have to say?"

"Perhaps your detectives can offer some proof."

"It's all here," he said. "Five times you predicted the return of the Kabaka. Seems you're getting mixed up in our politics, doesn't it?"

"Not me," I answered. "I stick strictly to the Bible in all my presentations. There is nothing about the Kabaka in the Bible."

"I thought I knew you Adventists," he said, "and I've never knew you chaps to meddle in governmental affairs."

"Nor do we take kindly to state intrusions on religion," I interjected.

"Yes, yes, I know," he answered reflectively, softening a bit. "But can you think of anything you may have said that may have given my detectives the impressions that they got? I've had three of them on you since you landed here."

Then it hit me. "Inspector, for three nights I have been speaking on the second coming of Christ," I said. For forty-five minutes I summarized my sermons. Why miss the opportunity? If the inspector was bone dry, he got a good dose of "living water" that day. As I grew animated, his fascination grew. He dropped his pen and listened attentively.

"When you said in your sermons 'Jesus is coming back,' did you ever call Him king?" he asked at the end.

"Yes, many times, King of kings and Lord of lords," I answered.

"That's the answer," he said. "Every time you said king, your translator said Kabaka. It is the only word for king in their language. When you said King of kings, your translator said Kabaka Abba Kabaka. Keep up the good work, teacher. If you have any problem while here, you have a friend in this office."

It is a policy in Africa to hold public meetings and hold Africans in baptismal classes for two years before baptizing them.

"Why?" I asked of church leaders.

"We must be sure that the candidates are free of heathenish practices before baptism," the church explained. I noticed that Whites in Africa were baptized on the profession of their faith—no delay. I resolved to change it. Two weeks before baptism, the president of the division suddenly appeared at the mission compound.

"Brother Cleveland," he said at breakfast, "I hate to disappoint you, but you won't be able to baptize your candidates. They must faithfully attend classes for two years before baptism. That's division policy, you know."

"I understand," I said, and continued eating.

"Any questions, Brother Cleveland?" he asked.

"None whatsoever," I answered. Satisfied, he left town the next day.

"Are you going ahead with the baptisms?" Pastor Muderspach, the Norwegian Mission president, asked me later.

"I have been commanded by my Lord to teach and baptize. There is no church policy between the words 'teach' and 'baptize' in Matthew 28:19, 20. For nine long weeks, I have taught. I will take them to the water in baptism."

To my surprise, Muderspach was delighted with my answer. "I'll construct a new baptismal pool in front of the church," he said. "And I will fill it with water. But I cannot help you with the baptism," he added. I was delighted. On baptism day, 108 precious souls were immersed in water in the name of Jesus Christ. Among them was the crown Prince of Uganda and many professionals. But something larger had taken place. The two-year "waiting period" for Black Africans *was demolished*. In consequence, thousands of Africans have entered the church. The saints are happy. The church rolls on.

15

Detroit, 1966

The General Conference of Seventh-day Adventists gathered in Detroit for officer election and other business. This world body had been in town three days without press acknowledgment. The editor of the *Detroit Free Press* informed the General Conference Public Relations Department that there would be no press coverage until they talked with some Negroes in the movement. The PR head asked me to go with him.

"I'm glad to see you, Pastor," the editor of the *Free Press* said. "Are they treating you any better than they were?" He picked up some newspapers to show me as he asked.

"We have a biracial commission in our church that has totally desegregated it," I told him. "But integration is an ongoing thing."

"What about those nine segregated conferences?" he asked.

"What segregated conferences?"

"Those nine Black conferences," he said.

"So they are segregated because they are Black. You have a problem? Why didn't you call the sixty-one White-controlled segregated conferences?"

Puzzled, he put down his pen. "You've got me there. Please explain it yourself."

"Gladly," I replied. "These nine conferences, though Black-controlled, include Caucasian, Asian, Hispanic, as well as Black members, and are open to all. The sixty-one White-controlled conferences have Black, Hispanic, Asian, as well as European constituents. Every institution has been desegregated by church policy. Blacks serve at every level of the church, administrative, and otherwise."

"But Dr. King says that there must be a proportionate mix to qualify," the editor argued.

"But Dr. King pastored a Black church," I answered. He threw in the towel. "Ours is a mix of self-determination and desegregation," I added. "The majority of Blacks have no appetite for the White cultural worship style. So the Black church, born in slavery, will not go away. It is now, and has been, a refuge from the withering winds of social, economic, political, and spiritual alienation in our society. An organization can only remove exclusion and foster inclusion. The worship preference must be left to the individual. We do believe in freedom of worship."

This concluded our business. The editor granted full publishing privileges and wrote an article himself, characterizing the Seventh-day Adventist Church as "the most integrated church in America."

A church election that year involved my department. The department head was retiring, and I had seniority in the department. The church faced a dilemma. There had been no Black head of a department in its history, except the regional department which handled Black affairs. My eligibility was earned, my credentials impeccable. Further, the world leadership came to Detroit to put me in, and Black delegates were determined. Only my wife and I knew the reality of the situation.

The departing brother told me whom he was recommending, and he wasn't Black. Furthermore, the incoming president was personally committed to another person for the job. He wasn't Black. Third, since coming to Washington, I had been exceedingly busy in civil-rights matters in and out of the church. With pen and voice, I had been a part of every liberation effort the church had made since 1954. Some Whites are insecure around a Negro like that. Celia and I knew the score when we came to Detroit. Perhaps we were the only Blacks who did. We were never disappointed that another White brother got the job. I am a political realist. I was not let down. I was never *up*.

The process, however, might interest you. When the nominations for head of the ministerial association were held, my name was first nominated. No other name was put on the board for thirty-five minutes. Executives from across the earth made speeches. The unbelievable was about to happen, when an officer of the GC slipped out of the room. He conferred privately with the incoming president. He returned to the nominating committee with the president's preference. Not me.

The speeches in my favor went on as if he had not spoken. At this point, Richard Hammil, president of Andrews University, suggested that since I did not have a degree, it would be difficult for me to serve the university under those circumstances. His speech carried the day. The president's choice was nominated.

One problem, though, the president's choice did not have a good image among Blacks. They threatened to march on the convention floor. His name had to be withdrawn. N. R. Dower was elected to the post. I have never met or worked with a more Christian person, and we have remained firm friends to this day. Moral and always ethical, he insisted on our attending all social affairs in his home. Even when I was inclined to miss, he wouldn't take No for an answer. He is one of the great Christians of our time and loyal to his staff.

I was the scheduled speaker on the second Friday night of that 1966 church business session. Sitting in the audience of thousands that night was Dr. Kenneth G. Hance, major professor at Michigan State University. He had called Dr. Shaw, of Andrews University, and asked if I was scheduled to speak. When he learned I was on, he asked his friend to bring him to the service. During my sermon, he leaned over to Dr. Shaw.

"When is your university going to do something for that young man?" Dr. Shaw understood the "something" to mean the conferral of a doctorate degree.

"I'll get right on it," his friend replied, and he did. In the year 1968, I was commencement speaker and became the first Black man to receive the Doctor of Divinity degree from Andrews University. How did Dr. Hance become acquainted with me? In 1966, Dr. E. E. Rogers submitted his doctoral dissertation to Dr. Hance, who was his major professor. It was entitled "A Study of the Evangelistic Methodology and Preaching of Edward Earl Cleveland." Dr. Hance never forgot what he read. Though I never met him, I have never forgotten Dr. Hance. In fact, a few years later, a White Adventist preacher submitted his thesis to Dr. Hance on the history of evangelism in the Seventh-day Adventist Church. Dr. Hance refused to approve it until the author included a section on E. E. Cleveland and his contribution to evangelism in the Seventh-day Adventist Church.

In the audience on the night of my speech was an angry young Adventist science teacher who had witnessed the struggle over my nomination earlier. He was Dr. J. Price Pearson, of Daniel Payne College, in Birmingham, Alabama. This school is an affiliate of the African Methodist Episcopal Church. The school was established in 1893. Dr. Pearson approached Dr. Gregg, president of the school, with reference to awarding an honorary doctorate to a Seventh-day Adventist minister. He handed him my résumé. Dr. Gregg agreed to try. He would need the approval of two bishops and the faculty. He secured both, and I became the only Seventh-day Adventist preacher to receive an honorary doctorate from that institution. To this day, I highly prize my Doctor of Laws degree conferred by Daniel Payne College.

On February 25, 1993, I was inducted into the Martin

Luther King Hall of Fame of preachers at Morehouse College in Atlanta, Georgia. This prestigious award came with the submission of my résumé by Elder Walter Pearson to the dean of the college, Dr. Carter. In the year 1989, I was cited by the Alabama governor as "Alabama's Most Distinguished Black Clergyman." My only regret is that Mother and Daddy did not live to see the fruit of their toil, training, and prayers. They trained their three preacher sons to neither be elated by success nor depressed by failure, to embrace both as building blocks for the future.

16

Overseas

There was trouble in Indonesia. The Dutch were being deported by the thousands when we landed there.

"You had better stay off the streets," I was advised.

"Think I'll take a walk," I said. My skin color in my favor, I traveled to Bandung. The sculptured rice fields are one of the wonders of the world. There I met some great Indonesian preachers. My classes were conducted in the Bandung school. During recreation period, we played Ping-Pong. I was undefeated until a small boy timidly requested the privilege of playing me. I took him on. I didn't win one game from him. He sent me into retirement. Even now, when my brethren are playing the game, I remember the little fellow and turn to other pursuits.

I ran a public campaign in Jakarta. Hundreds attended. A large interest resulted, and the ministers received valuable training.

I was in Saigon right before the Vietnam War. The country had the war jitters, but the people were friendly. Once again I was cautioned against walking the streets alone. Disregarding the warning, I found the people open. Beautiful Saigon. I would remember it later. Then there was Bangkok, Thailand. Like Venice, Italy, many of its streets were waterways. Merchants plied their trade in boats. The gilded temples of Bangkok are a photographer's dream.

I remember the Philippine Islands, the warmth of the people, and the beauty of the country. I was offered a fruit that smelled and tasted like pig. I was informed jokingly that I would have to forego my honorary citizenship if I didn't eat it. My honorary citizenship was promptly foregone. I refused the privilege.

My stay in Monrovia, Liberia, was unforgettable. President Tubman was a most gracious host. I ran my meeting in the Centennial Pavilion. Thousands attended.

Then there was Accra, Ghana, a beautiful West African nation liberated by Kwame Nkrumah. His minister of finance was a Seventh-day Adventist elder named Bedamah. Nkrumah sent messages to his allies, smuggled out of jail on tissue paper, according to the legends that surround the man. The words chiseled in stone at the base of his monument "Seek ye first the political kingdom—and all these things shall be added unto you," remained to mock him as his own people drove him from office. My meetings there were held in the Baden Powell Centenary Memorial Hall. Pastor J. J. Nortey was a convert in that meeting. He became president of the Africa-Indian

Ocean Division and still is as of this writing.

I will never forget Bombay on the banks of the Indian Ocean. My meetings were held in a Hindu stronghold. I was not allowed to make an appeal for converts. Thirteen people joined anyway. The Cuban missile crisis happened while I was in India. There was an encroachment by the Chinese over the northern border. Bombay was in its path, and I was in Bombay. These two crises passed, to my relief.

Karachi, Pakistan, was a memorable stop. I deplaned there without a visa and found they are very strict. The tall, turbaned Pakistani who interviewed me discovered I had no visa and ordered me back on the plane. I appealed on every grounds possible, but it was useless.

"Get back on that plane," he ordered, "or I will put you on it."

Sadly, I turned. "I'm just a Seventh-day Adventist minister, and I was hoping . . ."

"Hand me your passport," he interrupted. He put it in his pocket. "Go on into the city and stay as long as you wish."

"What changed your mind?" I asked, shocked and sensing a story.

"Well, you people saved my life not long ago. I had an accident, and they took me to your hospital. You have a big one downtown. They didn't charge me for nursing me back to health."

Taking a taxi to the hospital, I walked in and spoke to the young lady behind the desk. "Hello," I said. "I'm the owner of the hospital and wish to inspect the facility. Get me the manager." She seemed convinced that I was a candidate for some form of confinement.

"Wait here, mister," she said, quickly disappearing. A White American appeared, approaching with caution, and recognized me.

"Cleveland, what are you doing way out here?" he asked, genuinely glad to see me. "How long can you stay?"

"Can you feed me three days?" I asked.

"You've got it," he said, and proceeded to line up my speaking appointments.

"I'd like to visit the Holy Land while out here," I said to him one day.

"Impossible," he said. "It takes six months to get a visa from the Egyptian Embassy." I urged him to take me to the embassy. I had a visa in three minutes. Astonished, the missionary wondered aloud at the miracle. I assured him that the Lord, with the color of my brown skin, was a big help. Later, when I entered Abdul Nasser's Egypt, my skin pigmentation helped again. While passing through customs, the inspectors were giving everybody a hard time. As payback for British Colonial Rule, when guards had delayed non-Europeans for the minutest excuses, the White folk were getting it now. I finally came to the checkpoint, the only non-White in the line. The Egyptian inspector put his mark on all of my unopened luggage, smiled, and said, "You may go, sir."

Startled, I stuttered my thanks and moved quickly through the line. When I looked back, the slowdown was on again, the bags of non-Blacks were subjected to the minutest scrutiny. Cairo was exciting. Visits to the Sphinx, the pyramids, and a camel ride filled my two days there with real wonder. The Egyptians were great hosts.

My flight to the Holy Land was uneventful. As we reached the Jerusalem airport, however, the thrill of anticipation mounted. I would visit the tomb of Rachel, Jericho, Bethlehem, Golgotha, the Garden Tomb, the Mount of Olives, and the Dead Sea. But nothing eclipsed the excitement of entry. Thousands of Arabs packed the airport when we arrived. Upon landing, I found that King Hussein was expected any minute. I was the only Black on my flight.

Now we were all herded into a small room with a large window where we could witness proceedings. The king learned to fly airplanes in Texas and was expected to fly his own plane from Aman, Jordan. Meanwhile, I approached the Arab guard at the door and asked him why I was not outside with my people. Once again my skin color stood me in good stead.

"Pardon our mistake," he said, ushering me out into the sunlight. Delighted with my good fortune, I moved easily among my Arab brothers, taking pictures. I took pictures of the famed Arab legion, the band, assembled dignitaries, and the cloud-bedecked azure blue sky. The king's jet plane streaked into view, flanked by two others. They flew over in formation, banked, and landed.

The king deplaned, reviewed the Arab legion, saluted the assembled officials, and headed for his limousine. I stood at the end of the red carpet facing him, camera ready. As he came closer, I clicked the camera, but it didn't click. I was out of film. I had wasted my film on side issues and was now

110 · Let the Church Roll On

face to face with the king, unprepared.

There is a lesson here for all who read this book. We may waste our life's resources on the side issues and stand at last before the King of kings unprepared. I have been entertained by kings, presidents, and governors of this world. But none of this equals the privilege of daily communion with the King of kings.

17

Oakwood College

I graduated from Oakwood College in 1941 and served as a visiting professor there from 1950–1977. From 1977 to this writing, I remain a lecturer in the Department of Religion at this school. This means that few, if any, ministerial students have escaped my ministry in the last forty-six years. During those years, I have taught *Dynamics of Christian Living*, *Evangelism*, and *Christian Broadcasting*. For years, Oakwood College ministerial students were sent to me for field training. Later, Andrews University sent many of their men. It was my privilege to minister to a broad cross section of clergy. For twenty-three years, I have served on the Curriculum Evaluating Committee of Andrews University and am one of its adjunct professors. For three months, I was a member of the Oakwood College Board. I was there just long enough to propose the establishment of a branch of the Harris Pine Mills Furniture, making a workshop at the college. With the help of W. R. Beach, this proposal carried. Many deserving students financed their education working there.

While at Oakwood, I headed the Department of Church Missions. This responsibility dealt with the student missionary program, which sends students abroad to serve in a variety of ways. Having traveled the earth, I was uniquely prepared to assist them in the orientation process. I was also the student "trouble-shooter" when racial problems arose.

One American official persuaded a Japanese official to request that no Black students be sent to his field. I protested this decision and was joined in this effort by G. Ralph Thompson, Black secretary of the General Conference. The officials in Asia were informed that they would accept all students or none would be sent. The issue was resolved.

A similar problem arose in Nepal. A Black Oakwood student wanted to go there. A White American wrote that Black students would not be compatible with the culture and would not be accepted by the Nepalese. I ascertained from the government that no such policy or practice was permitted in Nepal. I also protested this missionary's presence in Nepal to the Division office in India. Within a year, this person was no longer there. Meanwhile, the Black student and his wife went to Korea, building a distinguished ministry.

While at Oakwood, we established the NAACP branch on campus. It was designed to teach civic awareness to the student body. Adventist voting strength rose considerably after this. It was a high day for the campus when this organization brought the son of Robert F. Kennedy to the campus. The

Huntsville community turned out en masse to hear him speak.

It is my work in the classroom that has given me most satisfaction. The class in *Dynamics* reached 165 students, with more trying to enter. My department head decided that my survival was at stake and put a cap on the class. It was an act of mercy. Teaching this class has given me a deeper appreciation for, and understanding of, the everlasting gospel. *Christian Broadcasting* and *Evangelism* are the other courses that I teach. It has been a highly rewarding experience. I will do this as long as I am welcome and able to contribute. I will ever be grateful to Drs. C. B. Rock, Mervyn A. Warren, and Benjamin Reaves for these years of prolonged service.

18

The Gifts

For as long as I can remember, I have hungered for ultimate spirituality. Since six, I have been conscious of the Holy Spirit's presence. Spiritual growth has been my concern since my father and mother taught me to pray. Early on in my ministry, certain spiritual gifts became evident. Answers to prayers were startling and frequent. I knew then, but even more so now, that disciplined living and dependence upon God were requisites for the exercise of these gifts. My personal prayers became expressions of total dependency. This deliberate cultivation of God-consciousness has, through the years, found its fruitage in gifts divinely given. "Heaven came down and glory filled my soul."

In Washington, D.C., a baby, Bradham, was diagnosed blind by doctors at Johns Hopkins University. His tearful mother called my home in a state of shock at this information. "Come over here right now and pray for my son," she said. I called three other pastors, and we met at her house. We all spoke words of comfort to the mother and knelt in prayer. We laid hands on the baby's head and pleaded for his sight. Each preacher and the mother prayed. There was no startling manifestation in the mother.

"Let the doctor check him again," she said. The very next night my phone rang. "My son can see, my son can see," the mother shouted. Her expressions of appreciation were profuse. I had a prayer of thanksgiving with her right then on the phone and gave honor and praise to the only true Healer for having heard our prayers.

Mrs. Alma Blackmon has few peers as a choral director in the Seventh-day Adventist Church. Her insistence on preserving the majesty, simplicity, and sanctity of choral music, as well as its complicated varied harmonies, sets her apart from most and above many. A life-threatening malignancy attacked this good woman, and she was faced with a surgery from which she might not recover. I visited her bedside and pleaded with God for her life. Many others prayed for her. Her repeated public testimony cites my visit to her hospital room as the turning point in her miraculous recovery. God alone can heal sickness. Physicians and ministers are His earthly instruments.

Demonology has come center-stage in this century. The practices are as widespread as they are varied. From the cruelty of witchery to sophisticated hot lines, psychics ply their trade. I received a call from a conference president to go to a certain city. "The church is practicing demonology," he said. I arrived in the town and found the pastor and much of the

The Gifts · 117

congregation "under the influence." The problem was so widespread that mothers were "exorcising" the devil out of their children. I got a group of the deacons together and went from room to room in the church, praying a prayer for "the cleansing of the sanctuary."

They had been taught that lust is a demon. Anger is a demon. Hate is a demon, etc. I gave them Bible studies on demonology. From the Bible we learned that a demon is an angel, not a state of mind or expression of emotion. These full-scale beings are here because they were cast out of heaven. They may control men, but they do not inhabit them. When Jesus "cast them out" of people, they were cast out of their lives, out of their affairs. They no longer control or dominate us. The Bible does not suggest that demons enter our bodies. No intelligent being that has lived in heaven would be comfortable in any portion of our anatomy. There is no portion of the human anatomy that can contain an angel. In my Bible studies to the church, I read descriptions of angels from Daniel and Revelation. Such beings could not, and would not, live inside a human being. Theology from the Middle Ages located demons in the abdomen and sex glands. This is mere superstition. Demon control is internally exercised from an external source. Devils are with their victims, not in them. Devils need not inhabit to control. I taught them further that Christ has given men power over demons. One's faith can set him free. After three months, the Lord prevailed, and the church returned to normal. The Word of God became preeminent in the worship service, replacing exorcism.

I was sitting in my tent one day when a woman approached with a very large man at her side, her son. "My son is demon possessed," she said. "He walks by night and sleeps by day. One night I awakened, and he was standing over me with a knife. He cannot hold a job. The 'voices' tell him to run, and he leaves the job running. The Obeah man has exorcised him twice and the Catholic priest once, to no avail. Can you help us?" she pleaded. I gathered the forty-eight ministers around him, and we prayed earnestly that God would deliver him. Unknown to us, God healed him, and he returned to a life of normality. Through these years, I have seen hundreds healed and thousands saved to the glory of God.

19

Roots

Powerful forces in the world shape our lives. We cannot know them all—but they are there. The privilege of growing up with both a father and mother at home cannot be discounted. The security, inspiration, and guidance that it brings engenders great good. The blessing grows with the inspiration of great educators and what they bring to our lives. Of course there is the church and its spiritual uplift, pointing young lives upward to the stars.

But much of how far we go or how much we accomplish springs from our *own choices*. All men have a will which the devil *cannot force* and the Lord *will not* force. To this extent, the attitude will determine the altitude.

Early on, William and Eunice Cleveland taught their children the value and dignity of hard work. They were taught the value of worship and good education. Integrity, honor, and decency were and are the cornerstones of character. Reading was encouraged. The library of the Girls Preparatory School was our feeding place. History was our favorite study.

My father belonged to the Negro Voters League in the city of Chattanooga, Tennessee. He was a voting black citizen in the nineteen twenties. In those days, it was not easy. In fact, any form of political activism was viewed with suspicion if you were Black. Walter Robinson was the president of the Negro Voters League. We called him the "silver-tongued orator." He was the most powerful political figure in the city. Knowing my interest in elocutions, my father took me to the meetings. I was thus early introduced to the spirit of the non-violent movement for political change. Thus early I was subjected to the power of the spoken Word. The Black orator was a fixture in Black life.

We grew up in church. It was the center of our lives. My father was a church elder for as long as I can remember, my mother a Sabbath School teacher. To them and us the Kingdom of God came first. It still does. The building blocks were there from the start.

The call of God was imprinted on the face of my soul by the Holy Spirit—a call recognized early in me by the age of 6. Denominational endorsement would come later, much later. Some confuse the two. God alone *calls* His messengers. Denominations *hire*. God calls His messengers by three methods: original conviction, association, and direct confrontation.

The prophet Samuel was an example of original conviction. At an early age he received divine designation, knowing himself to be Jehovah's special messenger. His lifetime of service reflects that commitment. Elisha was called of God through his association with Elijah. The power that was Elijah's fell upon him double and he was sealed for life. The apostle Paul reflects the perils and privileges of direct confrontation. He bore in his body the marks of his confrontation with the Lord Jesus. But his ministry stands unparalleled in the annals of church history. None before or after Him did so much, for so long, with so little, as did this prophet-evangelist.

We who live in this century and do God's work may minister by the same power and are promised unlimited scope. Those who believe this will accomplish the *unbelievable*, witness the *miraculous*, and experience the *undescribable*. They "forget themselves into history." Such men "deny themselves" forbidden privileges and pleasures. Their lives are an endless litany of selfless deeds and conquests.

These messengers have little time to cherish negative thoughts of privileges denied and slights received, however real. They acknowledge no enemies—though enemies there may be. Without the influence of a contrary wind—would the airplane reach the skies? So the wind blows for us and against us. Hence we soar and sometimes struggle. How else is character developed?

Joe Louis was untested until Max Schemeling punched him out. The return fight was no contest. Louis was the uncontested master in pugilistic circles. So may it be with us all. The negatives are as essential to our development as the positives. These understandings inhibit bitterness, bitterness that will wither any vine.

122 · Let the Church Roll On

Finally, a man's view of the future is as bright as his connection with Christ is strong. If in the past and present the Lord has been our ever dependency, we would know that the God of the past and present is the God of the future. And He who gave Pentecost to the Apostles is giving it to us.

So let us press on till the road of east and west is free, till beneath the four winds of the heavens, light and truth are the possession of all mankind. And when the last song of the minstrel has died upon his ashy lips, and the sweetest number of the poet has ceased to charm his death-dulled ear, and the eyes of the astronomer be far too dim to chart the course of yonder worlds that sail on high with light and power, and when you come to lay down your life as a garment, outgrown and outworn, go not like the slave forced to his dungeon. But sustained and soothed by an unfaltering trust, approach your grave like one who draws the drapery of his couch about him and lie down to pleasant dreams.

20

Tell It!

Tell it on the mountain.
Tell it in the valley.
Tell it on the boulevard, street, and alley.

Tell it in the sunshine.
Tell it in the rain.
Tell it in the best of health or pain.

Tell it to the village.
Tell it to the nations.
Tell it to earth's remotest stations.

Tell it on the land.
Tell it on the sea.
Tell it wherever men may be.

124 · Let the Church Roll On

Tell 'em that Christ is coming soon.
Talk about it morning, night, and noon.

Talk about the living.
Talk about the dead.
Talk about the things that Jesus said.

Talk about the Temple in the skies.
Tell 'em when the dead in Christ shall rise.

Tell 'em how to live.
Tell 'em how to die.
Tell 'em how to give.
Tell 'em how to fly.

Talk about Jehovah's holy day.
Talk about the true and living way.
Talk about mankind's hopes and fears.
Talk about the God who dries our tears.

Tell it to the high.
Tell it to the low.
Set the hearts of men aglow.

Tell it till the hills shout forth their praise.
Tell it till the seas their anthem raise.
Tell it in the summer, spring, and fall.
Tell 'em that Jesus died for all.

Tell It!

Tell it to the rich.
Tell it to the poor.
Tell it to the people door to door.

Talk about the Man of Galilee.
Tell 'em how He died to make men free.

And when there's nothing else to tell,
Then talk about the devil, death, and hell.

—E. E. Cleveland

If you enjoyed this book , you would also enjoy . . .

Make Us One

by Delbert W. Baker, editor

At a time when technology has brought the worlld's populations together in a "global community," the forces of separatism, tribal warfare, ethnic rivalry, and racism seem to be out of control. Sadly, the church of Christ—and that includes the Seventh-day Adventist Church—has not been immune to these gospel-denying forces. Can we get back to the cross, where all men and women are made "one in Christ Jesus" (Galatians 3:28)? Where love overrules hate? Where peoples of every nation, kindred, and tongue embrace rather than retreat? Where reconciliation replaces repression?

The answer is Yes. The time is now.

This unique work provides a blueprint and a challenge for Christians to love each other and build relationships in the last days.

Order today by call 1-800-765-6955